D1242781

# THE SPEECH CLINICIAN
## AND THE
## HEARING-IMPAIRED CHILD

# THE SPEECH CLINICIAN
## AND THE
# HEARING-IMPAIRED CHILD

*Edited by*

## ROBERT L. COZAD, Ph.D.

*Chief of Audiology*
*Associate Professor*
*Department of Surgery*
*University of Missouri Medical School*

*With a Foreword by*

## WILLIAM C. HEALEY, Ph.D.

*Associate Secretary for School Affairs*
*American Speech and Hearing Association*

## CHARLES C THOMAS • PUBLISHER
*Springfield • Illinois • U.S.A.*

*Published and Distributed Throughout the World by*

CHARLES C THOMAS • PUBLISHER

Bannerstone House

301-327 East Lawrence Avenue, Springfield, Illinois, U.S.A.

© *1974, by* CHARLES C THOMAS • PUBLISHER

ISBN 0-398-02983-0

Library of Congress Catalog Card Number: 73-12631

*With THOMAS BOOKS careful attention is given to all details of manufacturing
and design. It is the Publisher's desire to present books that are satisfactory as to
their physical qualities and artistic possibilities and appropriate for their particular
use. THOMAS BOOKS will be true to those laws of quality that assure a good
name and good will.*

*Printed in the United States of America*
C-1

**Library of Congress Cataloging in Publication Data**

Cozad, Robert L.
    The speech clinician and the hearing-impaired child.

    1. Communicative disorders in children. I. Title.
[DNLM: 1. Hearing disorders—In infancy & childhood.
2. Speech therapy—In infancy & childhood. WV270
C882s 1974]
RJ496.S7C67      618.9'28'55      73-12631
ISBN 0-398-02983-0

# CONTRIBUTORS

Jack Bradshaw, Ed.D.: *Associate Professor, Director of Special Education, College of Education, Texas A. and I. University, Kingsville, Texas.*

Robert L. Cozad, Ph.D.: *Associate Professor of Surgery (Otolaryngology—Audiology), University of Missouri Medical School, Columbia, Missouri.*

Cornelius P. Goetzinger, Ph.D.: *Professor of Audiology, Department of Otolaryngology, University of Kansas Medical Center, Kansas City, Kansas.*

William R. Hodgson, Ph.D.: *Associate Professor, Department of Speech and Hearing Sciences, University of Arizona, Tucson, Arizona.*

Rollie R. Houchins, Ph.D.: *Associate Professor of Audiology, Hearing and Speech Department, University of Kansas Medical Center, Kansas City, Kansas.*

Donald J. Joseph, M.D.: *Professor of Surgery, Chief of Otolaryngology, University of Missouri School of Medicine, Columbia, Missouri.*

Jane B. Seaton, M.S.: *Clinic Supervisor, Department of Speech Pathology, University of Akron, Akron, Ohio.*

Jacquelyn Simms, M.E.D.: *Hearing Clinician, The Special School District of St. Louis County, St. Louis, Missouri.*

Lester E. Wolcott, M.D.: *Chairman, Physical Medicine and Rehabilitation and Associate Dean, Texas Tech University School of Medicine, Lubbock, Texas.*

Verna Yater, M.A.: *Supervisor, Hearing Clinician Program, The Special School District of St. Louis County, St. Louis, Missouri.*

# FOREWORD

FEDERAL AGENCIES and national associations, in an historical commitment to the handicapped, have established a national goal of full, quality services for each individual by 1980.

Recent court decisions have determined that handicapped children and youth not only have a moral but a legal right under the constitution to equal educational opportunities appropriate to their needs.

Results of several research studies between 1958 and 1970 have repeatedly reminded us that fewer than twenty percent of the 18,000 school districts in the United States provide comprehensive services for pupils with moderate to severe hearing impairment.

In addition, speech pathologists, audiologists, and teachers for the hearing impaired have continually voiced the need for earlier identification systems, comprehensive hearing conservation services, scientifically derived sequenced curricula, realistic professional/pupil ratios, and formalized program development, management and evaluation procedures for the hearing impaired.

Each of these objectives can be realized by 1980 through concentrated, mutual efforts of well-informed parents and professionals, federal and state agencies, and local school districts. The venerable educational cliché of *individualization* finally must become a reality in practice if the 1,200,000 children with hearing impairments are to experience maximum psycho-social adjustment and educational achievement.

The editor and contributing authors of *The Speech Clinician and the Hearing-Impaired Child* make a timely and vital scientific and educational contribution to the profession. Each writes from a personal experience of having worked long and diligently to provide individualized, quality services for many children

vii

who began their lives in a world of silence disturbed by distorted sound.

This text provides others with an opportunity to profit from expertise gained through advanced study and practical experience and is presented with the authors' hopes that the information shared can be applied in meeting the needs of parents and children who must cope with the debilitating effects of hearing impairment.

WILLIAM C. HEALEY, PH.D.

# PREFACE

THE HEARING-IMPAIRED child who attends the regular school usually has verbal communication problems which manifest themselves, most obviously, as *speech problems.*

As the speech clinician is the resource in the school who works with speech problems, he is usually given the responsibility of helping these students improve their communication skills.

The number of hearing-impaired students that the clinician may have enrolled in therapy is often surprising. This point was emphasized in a recent survey, by the editor, which revealed that of 176 speech clinicians sampled, 136 stated that they had hearing-impaired children enrolled in therapy. Each clinician was seeing an average of 6.2 hearing-impaired students.

Because the clinician's specialty is that of resolving speech problems, the speech (articulation) problem may, initially, be the sole focus of therapy. However, after working with the student a short while, the clinician may begin to raise questions regarding the nature of the student's communication problems and whether *speech correction* should be the major focus of therapy.

In an effort to provide the clinician with a source from which he may become more informed about the various aspects of the communication problems of the hearing-impaired child, this publication provides a broad coverage of those problems in such a way that the information is practical and can be applied directly to the clinician's therapy program.

Specific, in-depth information is provided (1) to give the clinician insight into the basic aspects of each area presented, (2) to suggest practical methods which can be used to quantify the primary difficulties in a particular area and (3) to offer approaches which can be used to resolve the communication problems of the hearing-impaired child.

For the practicing clinician, this book is intended to be read as a reference to particular problem areas, rather than from cover-to-cover. However, it is hoped that it will serve as a guide for the new clinician in understanding the communication and related problems of the hearing-impaired student.

The editor is deeply indebted to each of the authors who contributed his expertise, time, and efforts to this publication.

Appreciation is also expressed to Mrs. Ruth Wakerlin, Dr. Tom McMurray and the Dept. of Medical Illustrations, University of Missouri Medical Center, for their help with many of the illustrations in this book.

Encouragement given the editor in producing this publication by Dr. Donald J. Joseph, Chief of Otolaryngology, University of Missouri Medical Center, and the Missouri State Department of Education has been greatly appreciated.

ROBERT L. COZAD

# CONTENTS

# THE SPEECH CLINICIAN
## AND THE
## HEARING-IMPAIRED CHILD

# CHAPTER I

# A PHILOSOPHY OF HABILITATION
# OF THE HEARING-IMPAIRED CHILD

## Lester E. Wolcott

THE HABILITATION of the child is a field of endeavor almost unbearably overpopulated by *experts*. With all of the many opposing, at least confusing, forces of nature imposing on the child's growth and development, it is a wonder, if not a miracle, that this very complicated, little organism even survives to adolescence. At this point, additional forces and habilitative efforts are applied with great fervor because the child might do something bad which may adversely affect his whole future.

The existence of any sensory or motor deficit further complicates the already complex status of the condition known as *normal*. Unfortunately, the focus of attention on the abnormal tends to completely abate the normal forces in favor of pity, remorse, and concern for the handicap. In many instances, there is complete sacrifice of the factors necessary for the development of the vast remaining normal functions of the child. It is for this reason that a major emphasis on *habilitation* must be generated when any handicapping condition is detected.

In dealing with any handicap, major or minor, single or multiple, temporary or permanent, the clinician must develop a frame of reference for any treatment program on which he embarks. If one is to establish a program of habilitation or, for that matter, rehabilitation, the goal of the program must envision an optimum response to the environment in which the child must grow and develop. The response to the environment will, of course, depend on many factors: (a) the innate capabilities of the individual, (b) the quality of his environment, (c) the understanding and acceptance by his parents and siblings and

3

(d) the objectivity and ability of the professionals involved in his habilitation. These factors are operable with or without a handicap but take on special significance when functional impairment becomes a consideration.

The terms *impairment, handicap,* and *disability* must be carefully defined and understood if one is to develop a workable philosophy of habilitation. *Impairment* is a purely medical determination based on anatomic or functional abnormalities or deficits which remain after maximum medical restoration has been achieved and are considered stable and nonprogressive at the time of evaluation. Impairment is objective and quantifiable but may not relate to any specific degree of disability in a given individual.

Functional impairment, however, always results in a *handicap.* The latter condition is best described simply as an extra burden which the individual must overcome or circumvent to avoid a significant reduction of any specific functional ability.

The degree of *disability* may bear little relationship to the amount of functional impairment or the resultant handicap. It is merely an estimate of the lack of adjustment of the individual to the various physical, psychological, social, and economic factors in his environment.

In the case of the hearing-impaired child, there is an obvious functional impairment which can be identified and quantified. This inevitably produces a handicap of varying degree, proportionate to the hearing loss. One may assume that with appropriate definitive treatment, the functional impairment may be minimized, and with proper habilitative management, the handicap may be overcome or circumvented with minimal disability.

Optimal habilitation of the unimpaired, normal child requires the assistance of society as a whole and specifically parents, teachers, clergy, physicians, siblings, and others. So it is with the child with a functional impairment. The *addition,* not substitution, of a professionally trained individual to deal with the specific functional deficit is essential. Too often, the other members of the habilitation team are eager to turn all of their combined responsibilities over to the individual trained to deal with a particular handicap. This action is unfair to this team member and commonly spells disaster for the child who will, in most instances, develop a permanent, irreversible disability. The emphasis on physical, emotional, and social development must be at least equivalent to that for the unimpaired child. It is the role of the clinician or therapist to assist other team members in carrying out their responsibilities in spite of the existing handicap.

Obviously, the parents and siblings are the major determinant in the optimum habilitation of the child with impaired hearing. It is, therefore, essential that they become as knowledgeable as possible in regard to the handicapping condition. *They must know that all curative measures have been considered and that the determination of permanent, irreversible hearing loss has been established beyond reasonable doubt.* They must also be aware that those responsible for the health care aspect of the habilitation program will continually reevaluate the problem and be aware of new developments which may reduce the handicap or even lead to curative procedures. With this responsibility being assumed by the health-care professionals, the parents can concentrate their efforts on providing the home environment necessary to enable the child to overcome or circumvent his handicap and to allow his growth and development to proceed normally.

For the professional, a set of general principles for the habilitation of the child with functional impairment is necessary since he deals with many specific deficits. It is the general treatment program with special variations for the individual problems that enable us to do the superlative job of which we are capable.

The first principle by which we must be guided is that of *definitive diagnosis.* One must have, as nearly as possible, a definitive diagnosis in order to successfully carry out the other principles. Hearing loss is obviously not a diagnosis, it is a symptom. Substantial effort must be directed toward determining the basic reason for the existence of this symptom. In many instances, it takes time to reach this kind of specific diagnosis. It may be on the basis of observations of the habilitation team or the family that a definitive diagnosis can be made. This indicates the value of adequate notes containing the observations of the patient's activities, condition, and pertinent statements throughout the periods of observation. These notes may provide the information necessary to establish the diagnostic determination necessary for an accurate *why* and a good habilitative program.

The second principle of habilitation is that of *prevention of secondary disability*. Early recognition of the problem and a preliminary plan of treatment is essential in this regard. In spite of the importance of definitive diagnosis, efforts to deal with the symptom of hearing loss should not be delayed. Measures to alleviate the handicap most likely need to be instituted early and be continued throughout the duration of the handicap.

The third principle is the *development of functional abilities*. One must capitalize on the existing abilities and perhaps develop these abilities more intensively than usual to insure maximum utilization of compensatory mechanisms. The tendency to focus on the impaired function at the expense of the remaining normal functions must be avoided.

The fourth principle is the *preservation of the dignity of the individual*. In order to achieve maximum habilitation potential, one must earn the confidence and trust of the child and his family. Even more important is the assistance one can provide in enabling the handicapped child to develop self-respect and confidence in his abilities. All of the people involved with his growth, development, and treatment must be constantly reminded of the serious consequences of actions and remarks which may destroy his dignity and delay the development of self-respect and self-confidence.

A sound philosophy based on accepted principles will allow the clinician to contribute significantly to the total habilitation of the child and not only to the specific handicap for which the clinician is trained. The early recognition of abnormal factors impinging on normal growth and development provides an opportunity for redirection of the total effort. Many of the difficulties to be encountered can be anticipated and consequently avoided. It is this functional opportunity which requires a sound philosophical base for those in the major disciplines associated with management of the hearing-impaired child. Training programs must reflect the holistic approach to treatment. With this approach and the innate dedication of the health-care professionals, major inroads in the habilitation programs for hearing-impaired children are imminently possible.

# CHAPTER II

# HEARING CONSERVATION AND THE CLINICIAN

### Robert L. Cozad

THE IDENTIFICATION of hearing-impaired students is usually made by a hearing screening program. Frequently, it is the clinician himself who detects the hearing impairments because he is responsible for conducting the screening program.

This chapter segments various aspects of a school hearing conservation program and offers suggestions to the clinician for the organization and conduction of such a program. Among the various aspects of the program considered are the following: (1) responsibility for initiating the program; (2) comprehensiveness of the screening program; (3) screening tests; (4) screening audiometer; (5) screening test criteria; (6) test environment; (7) program organization; (8) referral and follow-up procedures; (9) records; and (10) preventive education.

## RESPONSIBILITY FOR INITIATING THE PROGRAM

The responsibility for initiating a hearing conservation program is usually taken by a local school district. Although a few states do operate programs for schools, the traditional role of a state has been that of providing a special consultant housed in its department of health or education.

The consultant's role is usually that of advising local schools regarding funds for program development and technical matters related to the screening program.

Typically, the consultant cooperates with local schools in obtaining special education programs for those students whose hearing loss is severe enough to interfere with their education in the conventional classroom.

In brief, it is the responsibility of the local school district or

8

clinician to initiate the hearing conservation program, but some financial, organizational, and technical help is usually available from a special consultant in the various state departments of health or education.

## COMPREHENSIVENESS OF THE SCREENING PROGRAM

In the initial planning of a screening program, the clinician should consider how comprehensively screening will be done. Four questions which should be considered regarding this aspect of the program are as follows: (1) Should a selected portion or the entirety of each class be included in the screening program? (2) How inclusively and frequently should the various grades be screened for hearing loss? (3) Should those students who fail the screening test in the previous year's program be automatically included in the following year's screening program? (4) And what should one do about new students who enter the school after the annual screening program has been conducted?

### Screen a Selected Portion or the Entire Class

Recommendations for the selection of students to be screened have ranged from evaluating only those students referred by the classroom teacher to testing all students in the class. Research has demonstrated that teachers as well as parents correctly identify only ten to twenty percent of those students with hearing loss (Watson and Toland, 1946). In contrast, audiometric screening can identify ninety-five to one hundred percent. Thus, an effective hearing conservation program will screen all students from a class or grade level, not merely those suspected by the teacher as having a hearing loss.

### How Inclusive and Frequently Should Screening Be Conducted

Should annual screening encompass all students in the school or only particular classes? This question can be answered by considering the length of time the screening program has been conducted in the school as well as the relationship between grade levels and incidence of hearing loss.

With the initiation of a hearing conservation program, every student in the school should be screened. One will most likely find that the incidence of hearing loss is as great in the advanced classes as in the primary classes (Gendel, Cozad, and Schloesser, 1967). However, after an initial screening of the student body, one may then adopt a system which provides for periodic evaluation of selected grades in the following years.

Schools which have conducted comprehensive screening programs for some length of time report that the majority of hearing loss is found in the classes of kindergarten through third grade (Darley, 1961; Downs, Doster, and Weaver, 1965). Incidence of hearing loss is much less in the advanced grades, fourth grade level and above, primarily because of the early identification and resolution of hearing loss in the lower grades. Therefore, on-going programs have found that by concentrating efforts in the lower grades, much less screening is necessary with the older students.

In consideration of these aforegoing facts, many clinicians establish programs which screen the first four grades (kindergarten through third grade) annually, and more advanced grades once every two or three years.

### Should One Rescreen Last Year's Failures

One often hears it said that students identified in the previous year's screening program should be screened again the following year. Apparently, this suggestion is made in order to note any change in the hearing status of those students detected by the previous year's screening program. However, a hearing conservation program should seek, in cooperation with the student's physician, periodic hearing evaluations shortly after the student's referral and as often thereafter as necessary. This action would not permit an entire year's time to lapse without knowing whether medical treatment was helpful and educational procedures proper for the student.

### What Should One Do About New Students

A final point to consider is that of not overlooking hearing loss in students who enter school after the annual screening has been conducted. In today's mobile society many students enter school at various times throughout the year. Thus, it is highly desirable that a hearing conservation program have provisions to screen new students.

## SCREENING TESTS

Three hearing screening tests which have been most commonly used in school hearing conservation programs are the recorded speech test, the group pure-tone test and the individual pure-tone, sweep-frequency test.

### *Recorded Speech Test*

Screening was first introduced to the schools in the form of a recorded, group-speech test (Watson and Toland, 1946). This test required that the listeners identify spoken numbers presented from a phonograph record. To pass the screening test, one had to repeat the recorded material correctly until a specified level of attenuation was reached.

Periodically, the recorded speech concept is revised and advocated for hearing screening programs. Most recent forms have appeared as tape recorded tests. However, the newer recorded screening tests have not been widely accepted by hearing conservation programs.

There are several reasons for this lack of acceptance. First, most recorded speech tests present the disadvantage of often not detecting children who have hearing loss in the higher frequencies. This often occurs, in part, because of the limited frequency transmission of the testing instrument. Another disadvantage of the recorded speech test is that the equipment utilized for this screening test cannot be employed to quantify the hearing loss of those students identified by the screening program. Also, no practical time or efficiency advantage is gained by the use of recorded speech tests as compared to other types of screening tests. In brief, the recorded speech screening tests have not been viewed as advantageously as a screening tool as have been the pure-tone screening tests.

### *Group Pure-Tone Test*

Pure-tone screening tests are found in both group and individual form. The group pure-tone screening test, once a very popular school screening technique, involved assembling a relatively large group (ten to forty) of students in a classroom. Each student placed an earphone over the test ear. All the earphones were connected to one audiometer. This arrangement allowed the pure-tone stimulus to be presented concurrently to all members of the group. Upon the examiner's signal, the students usually marked a test form in a manner indicating whether or not a tone was present.

Although the group pure-tone screening test was initially thought to be an efficient method of screening, many factors have resulted in the decline of its use. Among some of these factors are the following: (1) Children below the third grade could not successfully take the test (Darley, 1961). (2) Not only was the multiple-earphone equipment employed by the group test expensive to purchase, but much difficulty was encountered in its calibration. (3) Upon completion of the screening, additional time was required of the examiner to score the test results. (4) The efficiency of the group test was really no greater than other methods of screening, for the group situation often resulted in confusion and misunderstandings, which caused many normal children to fail the screening test. And (5) if not carefully controlled, the group testing situation permitted the student with a hearing loss to observe the responses of normal hearing students and respond appropriately to the test. Thus, from the aforementioned discussion, one can understand why the group pure-tone screening test has declined in usage by clinicians.

### Individual Pure-Tone, Sweep-Frequency Test

The screening test most widely used by clinicians today, is the individual pure-tone, sweep-frequency test. This test involves sampling the ability of the individual student to hear and respond to several different pure-tone signals which have been chosen to evaluate his hearing sensitivity.

The individual pure-tone, sweep-frequency screening test has the advantage of permitting direct contact between the examiner and student during the test. This situation permits close observation of the student and his response to the test. The individual observation provides control over the testing situation and promotes valid results. Failure of the screening test is known immediately by the examiner. The equipment used for the individual screening test can be employed to quantify hearing loss without any modification or additional expense. Also, the individual pure-tone, sweep-check procedure may be successfully employed with students from kindergarten through high school.

With a well organized program, the individual pure-tone sweep-frequency screening test has proven to be as effective and efficient as any known hearing screening procedure. Therefore, it is highly recommended for use by school hearing conservation programs.

## THE SCREENING AUDIOMETER

The audiometer is the evaluative tool of the hearing conservation program. Ordinarily, this instrument serves not only as a screening device but as a tool to quantify hearing loss. Therefore, in selecting a machine, one should realize that the functional capability of this instrument should be broad enough to encompass the frequency and intensity criteria used in both the screening and subsequent evaluative tests.

### Instrument Capability

The audiometer purchased by a clinician should be capable of screening at several discrete frequencies and over a range of intensity levels. Specifically, it is recommended that the audiometer be capable of testing at octave pure-tone intervals from two hundred fifty Hz through eight thousand Hz. The intensity control, hearing threshold level dial, of the instrument should have a range of one hundred ten decibels in steps of at least five decibels (American National Standards Institute, Specifications for audiometers, 1970). An audiometer which meets the aforementioned criteria will not only allow one to select the desired frequency and intensity screening criteria but will permit one to quantify the hearing loss of those students who fail the screening test.

Bone conduction and speech reception threshold tests are highly desirable diagnostic procedures to have included in a hearing screening program. However, the use of these tests, as a part of the audiometer's capability, will depend upon the knowledge and experience of the personnel connected with the screening program. In many programs, these two tests may be performed by a state or regional hearing consultant, as the tests require special knowledge, skill and experience to assure valid results.

### Instrument Calibration

Selecting an audiometer which will meet the screening and evaluative needs of a program does not insure the future accuracy or trouble-free performance of the instrument. Therefore, it must be constantly monitored to insure continued, accurate performance. Ordinarily, manufacturers recommend that an audiometer be recalibrated every two to three years of normal use. However, it is not impossible for the audiometer to become inaccurate shortly after its purchase, especially if the instrument has been mishandled (Thomas, Presler, Summers, and Steward, 1969).

One can employ a relatively simple technique to monitor the stability of the audiometer. First, when one receives a newly calibrated audiometer, he can do a threshold test on himself in a very quiet room. The threshold values from this test should be retained as a permanent record. Every time the audiometer is used for the screening program, the same examiner should again test himself and compare the results with his original values. A change of ten decibels or more at any frequency should be regarded as an indication that the machine is losing its calibration. Appropriate steps should then be taken to have it calibrated.

There are two possible pitfalls in the above described monitoring procedure. First, the self-administered test must be done in a quiet room, or the noise may shift the threshold of the listener, thus causing thresholds to differ from the original values. Secondly, one must have stable hearing sensitivity or any change in the threshold values obtained from the audiometer may not be attributed solely to the machine. Such differences could be related to a change in the listener's hearing.

In addition to checking the intensity calibration of the audiometer, one should also listen for distortion or noise in the puretone signal. Not infrequently, a malfunctioning tone-presentation switch, noisy hearing threshold level attenuator, or defective earphone cord introduces unwanted noise into the test signals. By early detection and resolution of such problems, accuracy of the testing program can be maintained.

## SCREENING TEST CRITERIA

The selection of the screening test criteria usually reflects the underlying philosophy of the hearing conservation program. Two philosophies currently exert the most influence on the selection of test criteria.

One viewpoint stresses that all ear pathology should be detected no matter how slight the hearing loss (Eagles, Wishik, Doerfler, Melnick, and Levine, 1965). The proponents of this philosophy support the use of stringent screening criteria.

A second philosophy asserts that the object of the screening program is that of identifying students whose hearing loss is sufficient to cause communication difficulty in the classroom (Downs, Doster, and Weaver, 1965). Therefore, screening criteria differs from that used by advocates of the first mentioned philosophy.

This chapter concurs that it is the primary goal of the clinician to detect students who may have communication difficulties in the classroom because of impaired hearing. Therefore, recommendations for test criteria in the following section are based essentially on this viewpoint.

Two facets of the pure-tone test stimuli must be considered for the screening test. The first is that of the frequency range of hearing that one should screen. The second is that of the intensity of the pure-tone signal which should be used in the screening test.

### Frequency

In considering the frequency criteria that will be used, the clinician must decide which portion of the frequency range he wishes to sample and how many different frequencies are necessary to adequately explore the selected range.

FREQUENCY RANGE: Since the primary purpose of the screening program is that of identifying students who may encounter communication difficulty, the pure-tone frequencies related to the understanding of speech are most appropriate to use for the test. Therefore, it is logical to recommend pure-tone frequencies from the range of five hundred through four thousand Hz. This range includes those frequencies most important for hearing speech.

NUMBER OF FREQUENCIES: Suggestions as to the number of different frequencies to be used in the screening test have ranged from as few as one to as many as eight. A monograph dealing with hearing conservation implies that there is no conclusive evidence to justify the use of the extremes of one or eight frequencies in the screening of students (Darley, 1961). This same publication suggests that four or five appropriately selected frequencies should be satisfactory in detecting students' hearing losses. Thus, it is recommended that the pure-tone frequencies of five hundred, and one, two, and four thousand Hz be employed as the frequency criteria of school screening tests. Not only are the four frequencies a manageable number in terms of testing time, but these specific tones adequately sample the frequency range important for hearing speech.

THE USE OF FIVE HUNDRED AND FOUR THOUSAND Hz: The use of five hundred and four thousand Hz as a part of screening test criteria has received some criticism. These objections should be mentioned as well as an explanation of why the writer believes that the frequencies should not be excluded from the test criteria.

First, with regard to five hundred Hz, it is sometimes mentioned that this frequency should not be included in the screening test because noise in the test room may be in the same low frequency range as the tone (Darley, 1961). The consequences of such noise could be the failure of normal hearing students because the noise would mask the five hundred Hz tone.

The writer advocates the philosophy that if the test environment is noisy enough to mask the test stimuli, screening should not be done. In short, one should not have to select or alter the test criteria because of excessive environmental noise. He simply should not test under such conditions.

The second objection relates to the use of four thousand Hz. The exclusion of four thousand Hz from the screening criteria or increasing the intensity of the tone at this frequency is some-times recommended. These manipulations apparently have been made because a substantial degree of mild hearing loss is often found in the frequency region of four thousand Hz. This type of hearing loss is usually assumed to be the result of noise expo-sure.

It is true that present medical procedures cannot reverse most noise-induced hearing loss. It is also true that mild hearing loss at four thousand Hz does not usually present an immediate com-munication problem. However, if noise exposure continues over a period of years, communication ability can be impaired. Thus, by early detection of hearing loss at four thousand Hz and by education of students as to the consequences of continued noise exposure, hearing loss may be prevented from ultimately reduc-ing communication ability. Therefore, the exclusion of four thousand Hz or increasing the intensity of this tone in order to by-pass assumably insignificant hearing loss is not consistent with a broad concept of hearing conservation.

SUMMARY: In summary, the use of five hundred, and one, two, and four thousand Hz to sample hearing sensitivity should pro-vide an adequate number of frequencies, over a sufficient range of hearing, to detect deficiencies which might impair the educa-tional achievement of students. Therefore, the aforementioned frequency criteria are recommended for use by the clinician in his hearing screening program.

*Intensity*

As was previously noted, the criteria for intensity of the pure-tone stimuli must be specified at each test frequency. Thus, it is recommended that one screening level (hearing threshold level dial setting) be used for all frequencies and that this level be ten decibels, relative to the American Standard Association, 1951 audiometric norm.

HEARING LOSS DIAL SETTING FOR SCREENING: The choice of the ten dB (ASA) screening level can be related to the fact that a hearing level of fifteen dB (ASA) represents a level of hearing sensitivity at and beyond which students begin having difficulty hearing speech (Darley, 1961). By the use of a ten dB (ASA) screening level, students with fifteen dB or more hearing loss at any of the speech related frequencies should be detected.

RELATIONSHIP OF ASA TO ISO NORM: An addendum should be made in order to clarify the relationships of screening levels when one uses an audiometer calibrated to the International Standards Organization, 1964, audiometric norm (ISO), and the even more recent American National Standards Institute, 1969 (ANSI) norm, as opposed to one based on the American Standards Association, 1951 audiometric norm (ASA).

In brief, an audiometer calibrated to the ISO or ANSI norm has an intensity output of approximately ten decibels less than a compatible numerical hearing threshold level dial setting on an audiometer calibrated to the ASA norm (Guidelines for Hearing Screening Programs, 1965). Thus, one would screen at twenty decibels (ISO or ANSI) to approximate the ten decibels (ASA) screening level discussed in this section.

Audiometers calibrated to the newer ISO and ANSI norms are usually so labeled. Those older audiometers based on the ASA norm usually do not carry a norm specification on the face of the machine.

### Criteria for Failure

Failure to respond to the ten dB (ASA) or twenty dB (ISO or ANSI) tone at any one frequency in either ear should be considered as a failure of the screening test. This same criteria should apply to the results from a rescreening test.

Failure of the second screening test is justification for an evaluation of hearing with as many diagnostic tests as are necessary to establish the nature and degree of the hearing loss.

Hopefully, the state hearing consultant or the clinician can apply the necessary evaluative tests and refer students on the basis of these tests rather than simply refer on the pass-fail screening results.

Programs which have no special consultants available often refer students for medical evaluation on the basis of failure of the screening test. One should realize that this referral method is not the most desired method, for it can result in referral of many children who have no hearing difficulty. Referral on the basis of only screening results has primarily been used because skilled personnel were not available to perform complete evaluative hearing tests on those children who fail the screening test.

## THE TEST ENVIRONMENT

A problem frequently encountered in hearing screening programs is that of finding a noise-free test site. Excessive noise in the test room can cause normal-hearing students to fail the screening test by preventing them from hearing the test stimuli. If normal-hearing students are referred for medical evaluation on the basis of inaccurate screening results, fruitless referral and follow-up work is created for the screening program. Also, parents not only become unnecessarily anxious and concerned because their children are labeled as having a hearing loss, but parents are required to put forth expenditures for unnecessary medical evaluations. The examining physician may also become dubious of the competency of a screening program which refers normal-hearing students. Thus, one must have a quiet test area to insure that noise does not prevent normal-hearing students from passing the screening test.

The first step in obtaining an adequate test site is that of educating the school administration about the importance of a quiet test area. The second step is that of locating an area in the school which will meet the noise level and space requirements. In some instances lack of low noise levels and space may necessitate providing special test facilities before the program can be conducted.

### *Educating the School Administration*

Convincing the school administration of the need for a quiet test area involves explaining the fact that interruptions from noise prolongs the length of the testing program and keeps students away from class activities longer than ordinarily would be necessary. It also should be emphasized that normal students can be mistakenly labeled as having hearing loss if noise levels in the test area are too high.

### Selecting the Test Site

With the cooperation of the school administration, the clinician can usually find one or more sites in the majority of schools which meet or exceed the necessary noise-level criteria for conducting hearing testing (American National Standards Institute, Criteria for background noise in audiometer rooms, 1960). In many schools, the stage adjacent to the gymnasium has been found to be an excellent area for testing. Another often acceptable area is the music or band room. Either of the aforementioned areas is usually isolated from the majority of school activities and has some form of sound treatment. These areas are ordinarily spacious enough to accommodate a sizeable group of students as well as examiners and test equipment.

### Noise Levels in the Test Room

To determine whether or not the noise level in the screening area is low enough to permit hearing testing, sound level measurements can be made. The readings should be taken under conditions similar to those which would exist during the screening program. A noise-level evaluation is often available from a hearing conservation consultant from a state health or education department.

### Alternatives to Using Existing School Facilities

In instances where the noise level cannot be controlled, it may be wise to install a commercially manufactured acoustic (sound proof) room. However, if an acoustic room is necessary, it may be more practical to use a mobile testing unit equipped with acoustic rooms rather than a stationary installation (Cozad, 1966). Mobile units are not restricted to one school building. An added advantage is that such a unit does not demand space in an already crowded school. However, the program which considers acquiring a mobile screening unit should have a large enough school population to permit the unit's year-around operation in order to justify the large investment in the equipment.

## PROGRAM ORGANIZATION

The successful operation of a hearing screening program is dependent upon careful organization. Two general aspects of the program which must be well planned are (1) an informational program for parents, physicians, and school staff and (2) the procedures of the actual screening program.

### Informational Program

Organizing the informational program involves planning the distribution of facts relating to the purpose of the screening program; how the program functions; when the program will occur; and the value of the program to the school and community.

A somewhat different emphasis may be placed on information presented to parents, physicians, and school staff.

INFORMING PARENTS: Informational material for parents should highlight facts which relate to the purposes and benefits of the screening program. Parents should also be informed how they will be notified regarding the test results and, in general, what recommendations will be made for students found to have hearing loss.

Several different media should be used in presenting the information, i.e., personal presentations, newspapers, radio, T.V., etc., so that the majority of the parents will be informed.

Preparing parents in advance of the screening program rewards the clinician by increasing understanding and cooperation of parents when they are later asked to seek help for their children.

INFORMING PHYSICIANS: Discussions with individual physicians or presentations to the local medical society *must* be conducted so that all physicians in the community will be aware of the program and understand its purpose. These presentations also permit the physicians an opportunity to acquaint themselves with the person who is responsible for the screening program.

Information for the physicians should stress the goals of the screening program, specify dates of the screening and note that the physicians will be receiving requests for medical evaluation of hearing loss shortly after the beginning of the program.

INFORMING THE SCHOOL STAFF: Planning an orientation program for the school staff is also necessary in order to gain their cooperation. Presentations to this group should emphasize, in a positive manner, why such details as completing test forms in advance of the screening, releasing students from class upon request, and maintaining quiet conditions in and around the testing area are important.

If the staff receives the proper orientation, it will not only assure optimum conditions for the identification of students with hearing loss but will also contribute greatly to the speedy completion of the screening program.

### Planning the Actual Screening Program

Equally as important as organizing the information program is that of planning how the screening program will be conducted. Organizing the testing program helps assure accurate evaluation of the maximum number of students in the shortest possible time with minimum disruption of the school routine.

The following areas of planning should be considered in order to attain the aforementioned goal: (1) an efficient method of moving students to and from the test area; (2) the test setting; (3) rescreening of students; (4) a simple, accurate system of recording test findings; and (5) a coordination of all activities of the program.

MOVING STUDENTS TO AND FROM THE TEST AREA: A constant, orderly flow of students to and from the test area is important for the operation of an efficient program.

One may maintain a steady flow of students by using a rather simple technique. At the initiation of daily screening, twice the number of students should be brought to the test area as can be accommodated in the test room. Half of this group can be screened while the remaining portion waits. Upon completion of the first half of the group, these students can be returned to the classroom. By the time the remaining half of the group has been screened, runners can return to the test area with a second group of unscreened students, similar in size to the group previously returned.

This procedure of returning a group of tested students and retrieving an unscreened group, while a third group is being screened permits rapid evaluation of the entire student population.

THE TEST SETTING: With regard to the screening process, it should be made clear that although several students may be taken into the test room, screening is conducted individually with the pure-tone, sweep-frequency test. The presence of several students in the room permits the examiner to instruct a number of students at one time. It also gives students an opportunity to observe classmates take the test. This experience not only supplements and reinforces the examiner's instructions but may quell the anxiety of younger students who are sometimes apprehensive about the screening procedure.

RESCREENING: Rescreening of those who fail the initial hearing test is important. It is not unusual for as many as fifteen to twenty percent of those who fail the initial screening test to pass a second screening test (Melnick, Eagles, and Levine, 1964).

Rescreening should be organized and conducted in a manner similar to that used for the primary screening test. It is usually more efficient to complete all of the initial screening tests before undertaking the rescreening.

If all initial screening is completed in one day, then rescreening should begin the same day or as soon thereafter as possible. When conducted in the aforementioned manner, the screening program is completed quickly and places a minimum burden on the school routine.

SYSTEM OF RECORDING SCREENING RESULTS: A second consideration in the organization of the screening program is that of recording the test findings. An accurate, simple tabulation system must be maintained during the screening process in order to provide a record of those students who have passed and failed.

The recording procedure should be simple so that it does not impede the speed of the screening procedure, yet it must be accurate and complete.

One method of organizing and recording screening test results is that of having class rosters prepared in advance of the testing. An example of a roster form is seen in Figure 2-1.

A slip of paper should also be prepared for each student with information which corresponds to that found on the roster. An example of a letter informing the teacher of how to prepare the slips is seen in Figure 2-2.

CLASS ROSTER FOR HEARING SCREENING PROGRAM

Please type or print clearly. Record the entire class. If a child is absent on the day of the test, check this in the appropriate box below. Use a separate class roll form for each grade.

Date_____     School_____

Grade_____     Teacher_____

| | PUPIL'S NAME | | | Absent | Age | Sex | Test Findings |
|---|---|---|---|---|---|---|---|
| | Last, | First | Initial | | | | |
| 1. | | | | | | | |
| 2. | | | | | | | |
| 3. | | | | | | | |
| 4. | | | | | | | |
| 5. | | | | | | | |
| 6. | | | | | | | |
| 7. | | | | | | | |
| 8. | | | | | | | |
| 9. | | | | | | | |
| 10. | | | | | | | |
| 11. | | | | | | | |
| 12. | | | | | | | |
| 13. | | | | | | | |
| 14. | | | | | | | |
| 15. | | | | | | | |
| 16. | | | | | | | |
| 17. | | | | | | | |
| 18. | | | | | | | |
| 19. | | | | | | | |
| 20. | | | | | | | |
| 21. | | | | | | | |
| 22. | | | | | | | |
| 23. | | | | | | | |
| 24. | | | | | | | |
| 25. | | | | | | | |
| 26. | | | | | | | |

Clinician                    Audiometer

Figure 2-1. Class roster form.

Dear Teacher:

In order to maintain your regular classroom schedule and speed the process of hearing testing it may be helpful to reacquaint you with the general sequence of the program that we discussed earlier.

First you will receive, with this letter, a class roster form which may be partially completed before the day of the screening. Be sure to take the attendance on this sheet the day your class is tested. Absentees can then be tested at a later time.

A name slip for each child is the second piece of information needed. Be sure each student has a completed name slip before he is sent to the test area. These slips will have to be made by you or your students. To do so, take a sheet of paper and divide it into slips. Each child should have his name, grade, age, sex, and a blank space on a slip. Please see that this information is printed clearly or typed. Each child should hand his own completed slip to the examiner when he is tested.

Example of name slip:

| Last | First | Initial | Grade | Age | Sex | |
|------|-------|---------|-------|-----|-----|---|
| Jones | Tommy | L. | 2 | 7 | M | |

A monitor, either a parent, older student, or teacher, will serve to transfer the students from the classroom to the unit. A group of students will be taken to the test area at one time.

Upon completion of the test, the children will be returned by the monitor to the classroom.

Those children not passing the screening test may be brought back for more tests after the screening of all children is completed. These more extensive tests may take 30 to 45 minutes.

Thank you for your cooperation.

Figure 2-2. Information letter to the teacher.

Each student will take his paper slip to the examiner who records the results of the screening test on it. Upon leaving the testing area, each student deposits the completed slip with the person recording the test results. The findings from the student's screening test is then transferred from his slip of paper to the class roster as a permanent record.

If a student fails the initial screening test and is to be returned later for rescreening, his name slip can be retained by the recorder for further use.

In returning students for rescreening, the name slips have only to be sent to the classroom to obtain the desired students.

COORDINATION OF SCREENING ACTIVITIES: Suggestions offered in the preceding paragraphs will contribute little toward an efficient hearing screening program if movement of students, screening, and recording of results are not coordinated. In order to have an efficiently operating program, it is crucial that a mature adult supervise and coordinate all phases of the screening program. This person functions independently of the actual screening activities in that he does not do the moving of students, testing, or recording of test results. He simply coordinates all of the activities. Of all the staff members of the screening program, the coordinator holds the key to its efficient, successful operation by insuring that all phases of the program work together smoothly.

## REFERRAL AND FOLLOW-UP OF STUDENTS WITH HEARING LOSS

*The achievement of a hearing screening program in reducing hearing loss can be judged by the success of its referral and follow-up work.* If one expends the time and effort to detect hearing loss, he should invest no less time and effort to assure that it is evaluated and resolved. Thus, it becomes apparent that the effectiveness of communicating to parents, the fact that their child has a hearing loss which needs immediate attention, is critical to whether or not he receives that attention. Likewise, it is imperative to follow-up on student referrals in order to confirm the fact that they have obtained evaluation and treatment.

### Referral Methods

The method of referral often determines whether or not parents will seek evaluation of their child's hearing loss. The conventional method of referral is that of a form letter via the student to the parent. Experience has shown that many parents *disregard* this notice primarily because they do not understand hearing loss and its implications (Gendel, Cozad, and Schloesser, 1967).

The most effective way of communicating test findings to parents is by means of a personal conference. As time consuming as the conferences are for both clinician and parents, these meetings are time well spent in effectively convincing parents to provide an evaluation of their child's hearing loss. The importance and effectiveness of a parent conference cannot be overemphasized.

Parent conferences should provide an opportunity for the clinician to explain: (1) the fact that the child was identified as having a hearing loss; (2) the need for a medical evaluation of the hearing loss; (3) the possible implications of the hearing impairment if not resolved; and (4) the parents' questions regarding the findings and recommendations.

At the time of the parent conference, a medical referral form should be given to the parents. The form should include the student's hearing test results and a brief paragraph of re-explanation about the hearing screening program for the physician (remember you have already talked to all the physicians in the community).

A section of the medical referral form should be designed to be returned to the hearing program. This portion should also be self-addressed and pre-stamped. At the time of the medical examination, the physician can complete the form and return it to the school. The returned portion thus serves as an indication that the student did obtain a medical evaluation.

### Follow-Up Procedures

If no information regarding the child's medical evaluation is received from the physician or parents after a reasonable length of time, contact should again be made with the parents. One may find that financial problems, previously unknown, may have prevented the seeking of medical attention. Often, the parents or physician may have simply misplaced the evaluation forms, although the student did receive a medical evaluation. And not infrequently, a second discussion with the parents is necessary to convince them that hearing loss is a problem which should receive prompt attention (Gendel, Cozad, and Schloesser, 1967).

## RECORDS

Developing and maintaining a permanent record system allows one to determine the year-by-year effectiveness of the program in reducing hearing loss (Report of Committee for Hearing Conservation, 1959). It, too, provides information which can be used to project the type and extent of special education programs needed for that portion of the student population whose hearing loss is not reversible by medical or surgical treatment.

It is especially important that evaluation reports of those children with nonreversible hearing impairment become a part of their cumulative health record. For not only can one determine whether the hearing loss is progressing from year to year, but this information can be important for the student's future education or employment.

In brief, a well documented hearing conservation program is necessary to demonstrate the impact of the program on the reduction of hearing loss as well as facilitate the planning of special education programs for hearing handicapped students.

## PREVENTIVE EDUCATION

There is a great need for educational programs designed to inform students about hearing preservation. However, the value of preventive education in a school hearing conservation program is often overlooked because of the intense focus on the screening phase of the program. Thus, the potential of education as a tool for the prevention of hearing loss is not being fully utilized in the school program.

More educational programs should be evolved which teach the prevention of hearing impairment through the development of good personal health care. Emphasis should be placed on the importance of immunization against contagious diseases which can result in hearing loss. The importance of seeking prompt attention for seemingly minor ear problems should also be stressed. With emphasis on early resolution, the student can be taught that major problems can be prevented.

The dangers of excessive noise exposure and its effect on hearing must also be presented to students. The fact that excessive noise exposure can painlessly and unnoticeably cause permanent hearing loss is not a well-recognized fact. Teaching the necessity for the use of ear protection devices when exposed to potentially damaging noise will contribute enormously to the conservation of hearing.

If properly developed, the educational contribution of a hearing conservation program can be that phase of the program which contributes greatly to the long-term prevention of hearing loss.

## REFERENCES

American National Standards Institute. Criteria for background noise in audiometer rooms. ANSI S3. 1-1960. New York, American National Standards Institute, 1960.

American National Standards Institute. Specifications for audiometers. ANSI S3. 6-1969. New York, American National Standards Institute, 1970.

Cozad, R. L.: The hearing impaired student and the speech clinician. *J Mo Speech Hearing Assoc*, 4:7-13, 1971.

Cozad, R. L.: Mobile unit for hearing tests of Kansas children. *Public Health Rep*, 81:573-576, 1966.

Cozad, R. L.: A survey of hearing conservation programs conducted by public health and school nurses. *J Sch Health*, 36:454-461, 1966.

Darley, F. L. (Ed.): Identification audiometry. *J Speech Hearing Dis*, Monograph Supplement Number 9:1-68, 1961.

Downs, M. P., Doster, M. E. and Weaver, M.: Dilemmas in identification audiometry. *J Speech Hearing Dis*, 30:360-364, 1965.

Eagles, E. L., Wishik, S. M., Doerfler, L. G., Melnick, W., and Levine, H. S.: *Hearing sensitivity and related factors in children*. Graduate School of Public Health, University of Pittsburgh, 1965.

Gendel, E., Cozad, R. L., and Schloesser, P.: Hearing conservation for Kansas children: A cooperative project in preventive medicine. *J Kansas Med Soc*, 68:363-366, 1967.

*Guidelines for hearing screening programs: Calibration of audiometers*. U.S. Department of Health, Education and Welfare, Welfare Administration, Children's Bureau, 1965.

Melnick, W., Eagles, E. L., and Levine, H. S.: Evaluation of a recommended program of identification audiometry with school-age children. *J Speech Hearing Dis*, 29:3-13, 1964.

Osborn, C. D.: Medical follow-up of hearing tests. *J Speech Hearing Dis*, 10:261-273, 1945.

Report of the Committee for Hearing Conservation of the School Health Section of the American Public Health Association and American School Health Association. *J Sch Health,* 24:171-186, 1959.

Thomas, W. G., Presler, M. J., Summers, R. R., and Stewart, J. L.: Calibration and working conditions of one hundred audiometers. *Public Health Rep,* 84:311-327, 1969.

Watson, L. A. and Toland, T.: *Hearing tests and hearing instruments.* Baltimore, Williams and Wilkins, 231-267, 1946.

# CHAPTER III

# SOME MEDICAL IMPLICATIONS REGARDING THE HEARING IMPAIRED STUDENT

### Donald J. Joseph

IT IS THE INTENT of this chapter to identify and discuss some of the medical problems which are of importance in considering the hearing-impaired student. After reading this chapter, it is hoped that the clinician will have a better understanding of the medical diagnosis and treatment of his students.

The first step in habilitating the hearing-impaired student is that of establishing whether or not his hearing impairment can be resolved medically or surgically. Perhaps the clinician will be the one to note the hearing deficiency. If so, it will be his responsibility to contact the student's parents with the recommendation for a medical evaluation.

The referral and treatment process may sound rather simple, but at times it is not. It takes for granted that the parents are alert, intelligent, and concerned. It also assumes that the family physician will be able to determine the etiology of the hearing loss and treat it or will refer the student to an otolaryngologist. Often, the latter mentioned course of action is not always taken. Most general practitioners, or family physicians, are not well trained in every speciality. Thus, it may require a considerable amount of tact and gentle persuasion on the part of the clinician to bring about a thorough otologic evaluation.

## THE IMPORTANCE OF A ROUTINE PHYSICAL EXAMINATION

An ideal school situation would require that every student have an annual physical examination including a test of hearing. This physical examination is important because there are conditions, such as cholesteatoma or recurrent serous otitis, in which the hearing could be within normal limits from hearing test results and yet progressive ear disease could be present. A physical examination could identify such conditions.

At the other extreme or as a minimum requirement, any program aimed at identifying and educating the hearing-impaired student should require at least an initial physical examination prior to the student's entrance into school. Subsequent examinations should be requested if and when it was thought that there had been a change in the student's physical condition.

## CLASSIFICATION OF HEARING LOSS

There have been many different classifications of hearing disorders. It is not our purpose to go into any complicated classification. It is probably best that we utilize the well-accepted terminology of conductive and sensorineural loss. It is also convenient to refer to disease of the external ear, middle ear, and inner ear in relationship to the aforementioned types of hearing loss.

### Conductive Loss

Any condition which interferes with or blocks the transmission of sound from the external ear to the inner ear may result in a conductive hearing loss.

THE EXTERNAL EAR: The external ear is generally considered to include the auricle and external ear canal, as shown in Figure 3-1. Although important for hearing in animals, the absence or loss of the auricle in man presents essentially no hearing handicap. However, blockage of the external canal by (a) cerumen, (b) foreign bodies, (c) external otitis or (d) congenital abnormalities can result in varying degrees of hearing loss.

*Cerumen* serves as a protective coating to the skin of the external ear canal. Normally, it works its way out of the canal. Occasionally, however, it accumulates and becomes a problem. Firmly impacted cerumen can cause up to twenty-five to thirty decibels of hearing loss. When hearing loss is noted, often the position of the accumulated cerumen is more important than the amount.

It is not unusual to see conductive hearing loss in which a

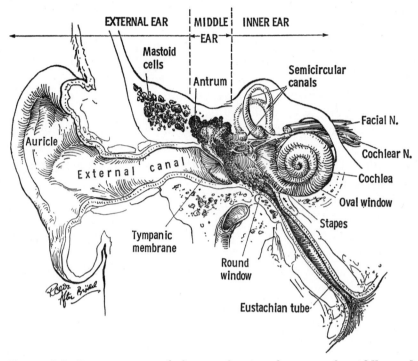

Figure 3-1. Basic anatomy of the ear showing the external, middle, and inner ear.

rather small amount of cerumen is lying against the drum, or a small amount is completely blocking the canal. On the other hand, one may remove copious amounts of cerumen from an ear canal in which there is no loss because there is sufficient air space around the cerumen to allow for adequate transmission of sound waves.

Although blockage by *foreign bodies* is most common in the child aged two to four years, it does occur in older students. Foreign bodies have been known to remain in ears for many years, unnoticed until sufficient cerumen has built up around them to cause symptoms of hearing loss. However, a foreign body does not cause hearing loss unless its presence leads to inflammation or cerumen accumulation with subsequent canal occlusion.

The skin of the external auditory canal is subject to the same disease as skin anywhere on the body. In fact, the ear canal is warm, moist, and is especially prone to flaking and itching. Cerumen helps to protect the ear canal from water and irritation, but many people lack adequate cerumen and many are great ear-scratchers. Children and young adults get bathed often, take many showers, swim, and get their heads under water at every opportunity. This increased moisture in the external ear canal leads to irritation of the canal skin. If the skin is scratched, bacteria are quick to invade and grow in this warm, moist area causing *otitis externa*.

Otitis externa is often painful, and there often is some discharge from the ear. Repeated episodes of otitis externa may cause hearing loss during the early stages of the infection because the ear canal may be swollen shut. Hearing loss occurring at later stages of external otitis usually is the result of the accumulation of considerable amounts of exudate or discharge from the disease process. Rarely, though, does otitis externa give a chronic or progressive loss, since it does not attack the middle ear structures.

It may or may not be possible for the clinician to look at a student and tell whether or not he has a *congenital ear deformity*. He may obviously have an external ear deformity and have perfectly normal hearing. On the other hand, the student may have a perfectly normal appearing ear and have a rather severe hearing loss. This is true because the hearing apparatus is formed in the embryo from several distinctly different structures. If only one of these structures is amiss in its development, then only that portion of the ear will be deformed. Fortunately, congenital deformities are not common, and when present, are more often unilateral.

In most cases of congenital external ear deformities, the inner ear is normal. This means that if there is some way of surgically making the conductive apparatus function, hearing may be restored. This surgery might entail merely opening up the bony external ear canal which is abnormally filled with skin and fibrous tissue. It might mean boring out or creating a new bony canal. It could entail replacing or repositioning some missing or misplaced ossicles. Obviously, if the ear canal is closed, or if there is a defect in the ossicles, a rather marked conductive loss is likely to be present.

There is no great need to rush into surgery when the deformity is unilateral, since the individual with normal hearing in one ear has little difficulty learning speech or functioning reasonably well in a classroom.

If the congenital external ear deformity is bilateral, an entirely different situation exists. The individual is handicapped with his bilateral conductive hearing loss. Since the inner ear apparatus is probably normal, most otologists would suggest that a bone-conduction type hearing aid be fitted immediately. By about age 3 or 4, the child would be able to cooperate well enough to give valid audiological test results. This would greatly enhance the success of surgery since one could be reasonably sure of the inner ear function and of any difference between the two ears. Also, the older the child, the more cooperative he may be in the postoperative care.

THE MIDDLE EAR: The middle ear has several different functions related to hearing. The two most important functions for the purpose of this chapter are (1) the fact that the middle ear conducts sound energy, by way of the ossicles, to the fluid of the inner ear and (2) by means of the eustachian tube's opening and closing, air pressure in the middle ear remains equalized with pressure in the external ear canal. This equalized pressure permits the eardrum to vibrate normally.

Middle ear dysfunction from (a) perforation of the tympanic membrane, (b) eustachian tube dysfunction, (c) inflammation and infection of the middle ear from acute, chronic, or serous otitis media are perhaps the most common problems causing conductive hearing loss in the student.

In order for the *tympanic membrane* to function normally, it should completely seal off the middle ear from the external ear; it should be firmly attached to the malleus; and it should be able to vibrate freely. These requirements have many implications. First and of most importance, the drum should not have a perforation in it.

A small pinpoint perforation may cause little or no clinical hearing impairment. A large one, occupying as much as half of the drum, may cause as much as twenty-five decibels of hearing loss. Obviously, perforations whose size varies between these extremes vary considerably in the degree of hearing loss which may accompany them. If the hearing loss accompanying the perforation is greater than twenty-five decibels, the otolaryngologist becomes suspicious that other factors such as ossicular damage may also exist.

Perforations may come about in several ways. Most of them are secondary to middle ear infections. Middle ear infections can cause drum perforations by several means. The infection may build up enough pressure from the accumulation of pus and mucus to cause the drum to bulge outward and burst. Also, the infection may directly involve the drum tissue, weaken it and cause it to break.

A lesser number of perforations are due to trauma to the ear. A blow to the ear by a hand, a blunt object or even a gush of water can build up enough pressure to blow in the eardrum.

In most cases, whether the perforation is induced by infection or by trauma, it heals spontaneously, usually within a week or two. If a perforation fails to heal promptly, the otolaryngologist may apply a caustic liquid such as silver nitrate around the circumference of the perforation. A tiny, very thin layer of tissue paper is then placed over the perforation. The liquid tends to make the circular edge of the perforation fresh or raw so that the drum tissue is given a chance to grow across and close the perforation. The paper gives the drum tissue a fragile framework across which it can bridge. This treatment quite frequently will close small perforations and occasionally ones as large as one-third of the drum.

When a large perforation exists or a small perforation persists in spite of several patchings, it becomes necessary to resort to surgery. When surgery is done to repair a perforation, instead of a piece of paper, a piece of thin human tissue is laid over the perforation and adjacent raw areas. This surgical procedure is known as *Type I tympanoplasty* or a *myringoplasty*.

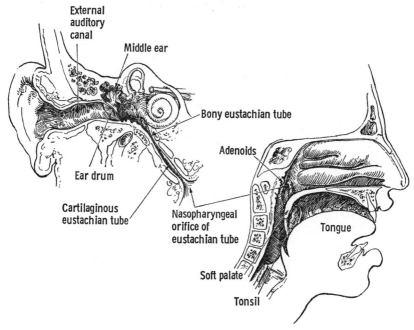

External
auditory
canal

Middle ear

Bony eustachian tube

Adenoids

Ear drum

Cartilaginous
eustachian tube

Nasopharyngeal
orifice of
eustachian tube

Tongue

Soft palate

Tonsil

Figure 3-2. The location, openings, and pathway of the eustachian tube in relation to the middle ear and nasopharynx.

In general, more than eighty percent of the perforation repairs are successful. Although some perforations require repatching, some do not heal after several attempts at correction. In the latter cases, there is often other disease or infection present in the middle ear which prevents normal healing. Often it is necessary to treat these other conditions to be sure the eardrum is ready for surgical repair.

The *eustachian tube,* illustrated in Figure 3-2, plays a key role in the functioning and well being of the middle ear. Its most important role is that of maintaining equalization of the air pressure in the middle ear cavity with that of atmospheric pressure. This pressure equalization permits normal eardrum vibration.

To maintain atmospheric pressure in the middle ear, the eustachian tube functions in the following manner. The inner opening of the eustachian tube in the nasopharynx is normally closed. But when one swallows or alters the position of the soft palate, the valve-like end of the tube opens. This opening permits air exchange between the middle ear cavity and normal atmospheric air contained in the oral cavity.

A malfunctioning eustachian tube can lead to several different types of ear disease. In addition, its malfunction is the major cause of the failures in middle ear reconstructive surgery.

Many factors can alter the eustachian tube's normal function. For example, one can surmise that if the muscles of the palate are involved in swallowing, then deformities of the palate might cause eustachian tube malfunction. This is true, and is best demonstrated by the well known fact that students with cleft palates usually have eustachian tube and subsequent ear problems.

One can imagine the problems that could also occur if there were some nasopharyngeal swelling in the area surrounding the eustachian tube's opening. This swelling might reduce the size of the tube's opening so that adequate ventilation of the middle ear cavity could not occur.

Swelling in the area of the eustachian tube's opening can be due to an infection in the nose or throat, or due to an allergy causing the membranes of the nose and nasopharynx to be swollen. This fact explains why so much attention is given to the nose and throat when ear infections are a problem.

Also, one can imagine that even though the tube seems to operate adequately, there might be some mass of tissue at the opening which would block it. The tissue blocking the tube may be adenoid tissue which has grown too large. It could also be some type of tumor. See Figure 3-3.

Infected sinuses, noses, throats, and tonsils can all spread their infections to nearby areas. It follows, then, that even though the eustachian tube is a normal functioning structure, it is a tube, and infections can spread up this tube to the middle ear.

It appears then, that the structures surrounding the inner end of the eustachian tube can initiate ear trouble by causing malfunctioning of the tube by swelling it shut. They can also

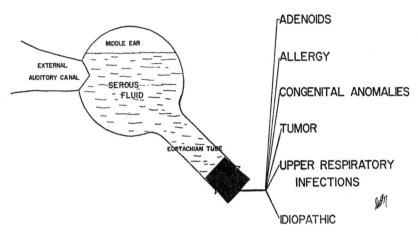

Figure 3-3. A schematic illustration of the *plugged-up* eustachian tube resulting in fluid accumulation in the middle ear space. The *plug* is composed of some factors which might cause blockage of the tube.

spread their infection up the tube to the ear. Either or both of these possibilities ordinarily bring about ear disease.

Whatever the condition causing the eustachian tube obstruction, it must be corrected. An allergic problem may need antihistaminic drugs to control it. Also extensive skin testing and a very elaborate evaluation of the student's contacts with foods, animals and other materials may be necessary to identify the cause of the allergy. If the tubal obstruction is secondary to a sinus or nasal disease then those causes must be treated. Some cases may require surgery, for instance, removal of hypertropied adenoids which are blocking the eustachian tube opening.

At times, nonsurgical therapy may control the disease. In some selected cases, the physician may suggest that the patient inflate his own malfunctioning eustachian tubes to maintain pressure equalization in the middle ear. By occluding the nose and attempting to blow away the fingers which are clamping the nose, air can often be forced up through the eustachian tubes and into the middle ears. Also, some patients are given a Politzer bag with which they can force air up through the nose and into the eustachian tubes. These methods of inflation are used only in selected cases, but they are often quite helpful in ventilating the middle ear.

Otitis media is a broad term signifying an *inflammation or infection in the middle ear*. It is usually classified as acute, chronic or serous otitis media. It is almost always accompanied by a conductive hearing loss.

*Acute otitis media* is a general term used to describe an ear infection which involves the middle ear. It develops rather suddenly, perhaps following a cold, and has all the characteristics of an acute infection. The student will be in pain, may have a little fever, and the eardrum will be red and inflamed. The hearing will be decreased by perhaps ten to thirty decibels of conductive loss, but an audiogram is seldom done because the patient is ill and in pain. He is quite unconcerned about the hearing loss. He needs medical treatment and should see a physician.

Antibiotic therapy will probably eliminate the infection. In addition, the physician might prescribe nasal spray or drops, and an antihistaminic-decongestant to be taken along with the antibiotic. The above mentioned medications are used in an attempt to facilitate the opening of the eustachian tube by decreasing the swelling in the membranes of the nose and nasopharynx. If the eustachian tube is opening normally, then any discharge in the ear might drain down the tube rather than building up pressure and rupturing the drum. If this type of acute otitis media is noted early and treated as described, there probably will be no pus formed since the bacteria growth may be halted.

When an ear with an acute otitis media recovers, usually the hearing returns to normal. It is prudent, however, to check the hearing a week or so after the infection subsides. If the acute otitis media does not respond to treatment or if the ear is not treated, the infection may continue to exist; the ear may continue to drain; and the hearing may continue to be poor.

*Chronic otitis media* may then develop. There may be very little pain involved in chronic otitis media infection since the drum is probably perforated and no pus pressure builds up. However, the ossicles may become eroded. Scar and granulation tissue may develop in the middle ear. Also, the various nooks and crannies of the irregular middle ear space may become involved in little walled-off infections. These low grade infections may persist for years.

In some cases, the skin from the external canal may grow into the middle ear through an eardrum perforation and form a pocket of skin cells. This pocket of skin cells is known as a cholesteatoma. It is dangerous, for it can continue to grow into the middle ear, expanding, invading and destroying the middle ear and inner ear structures. The cholesteatoma is often accompanied by a chronic ear infection and may have a foul smelling discharge.

Chronic suppurative otitis media and cholesteatoma often do not respond to any type of medication. Surgery may be needed to rid the ear of diseased tissue and to repair a damaged ossicular chain. The mastoid cells, a honeycomb-like collection of air-filled spaces inside the mastoid bone (Figure 3-1) communicate with the middle ear through one of the middle ear openings. Often these cells become infected, and much the same process of destruction can occur in the mastoid cells as previously described in regard to the middle ear. In fact, a smoldering, chronic infection in the mastoid cells may drain pus into the middle ear and keep it inflamed. The surgery then may involve just the middle ear space; it may involve just the mastoid cells; and it often involves both.

Surgical eradication of disease and repair of the ear in conductive losses related to chronic otitis media and cholesteatoma usually involves a *tympanoplasty* or *mastoidectomy*. There are several types of tympanoplasty. They range from a simple reconstruction of the tympanic membrane to a more extensive reconstruction of the damaged ossicular chain and middle ear. There are also several types of mastoidectomies. This procedure involves removal of varying portions of the infected mastoid air cells and often some or all of the ossicular chain.

*Serous otitis media* is probably the major cause of hearing loss in students with middle ear problems. It has been given many names over the years in order to more accurately classify it. It has been called secretory otitis media, effusion of the middle ear, catarrh of the middle ear, mucoid ear, tympanic hydrops, glue ear, and other terms. Regardless of the terminology, it merely indicates that the middle ear contains fluid that is impeding the normal sound conducting function of the eardrum and ossicles.

There are several mechanisms involved in the accumulation of fluid in the middle ear resulting in serous otitis media. In some cases, because of an allergy or a mild infection, the membrane lining the middle ear space may become irritated. The tiny glands in this lining may secrete more fluid than normal. The eustachian tube may not be able to drain away this excess secretion because it is too swollen from the same irritation. Fluid then accumulates.

A more common situation leading to serous otitis media develops from some disease process which occurs at the nasopharyngeal end of the eustachian tube. Let us suppose that one of the disease processes does exist, and the eustachian tube ceases to open normally. Air is then trapped in the middle ear space. Thus, when the middle ear becomes sealed, the tiny blood vessels in the middle ear lining absorb the air. This leaves a negative pressure, relative to the pressure in the external canal. The result is a vacuum in the middle ear. This accounts for the sensation of the ear's being plugged up.

A careful examination of the eardrum at that time might show it to be sucked in or retracted. This condition usually occurs over a day or two and is not usually accompanied by pain. An alert adult might complain of the sensation and seek medical help. A busy child, with this rather mild discomfort, might not complain at all.

Once this vacuum is present in the middle ear, several events can occur. If the eustachian tube begins to function again because the swelling in the back of the nose decreases, the eustachian tube may allow air to gain access to the middle ear. The vacuum would disappear. The drum then would move back to its normal position.

If the vacuum persists because the eustachian tube closure persists, another series of events can occur leading to a serous otitis media (illustrated in Figure 3-3). The mucosal lining in the middle ear, as was stated before, has many small blood vessels in it. This constant vacuum in the middle ear literally sucks fluid from these vessels into the middle ear space. Thus, the middle ear becomes partially or completely filled with this transudate fluid. Now, a serous otitis exists.

Thus, there are two ways in which fluid may collect in the middle ear. First, the fluid may be the result of an overproduction of mucus by the mucous glands in the lining membrane of the middle ear. Second, the fluid may be sucked into the middle ear from the tiny blood vessels which are present in that same lining mucosa. By far the most common situation is the latter.

Now that a serous otitis has developed, several possible events can occur. First, the eustachian tube obstruction can resolve itself. The cold or the allergy may get better. The eustachian tube might then begin to function normally. The fluid would drain through the tube into the back of the nose, and again all is well. Undoubtedly, most serous otitis cases resolve themselves in this manner.

If the serous otitis media does not clear up, then there are several possibilities to consider. Any body cavity which becomes blocked often becomes infected. There are bacteria present in our body at all times. Normally, our body has defense mechanisms which are able to keep an infection from developing. When the balance is upset by added irritation, or by poor circulation, or by poor drainage, these bacteria may grow and cause a true infection. A true otitis media can then develop with the characteristic symptoms of pain, swelling and redness. The infected ear is no longer said to have serous otitis, but instead has a true acute otitis media.

Two different end results have now been described. In the first, the serous otitis rapidly cleared up on its own. In the second, the ear with serous otitis became secondarily infected and probably required medical or surgical therapy. A third situation may develop which is perhaps the major cause for a conductive hearing loss in children.

If the serous otitis does not clear up quickly, and if it does not become infected, then it may remain for weeks, months, or even years. There will be no pain, no drainage, and the condition may manifest itself only by a hearing loss. It must be said that some cases of acute otitis media which are treated with antibiotics may clear up as far as the infection goes but still retain fluid. These cases present themselves in the same manner as a typical chronic serous otitis media. To assure that a serous otitis condition does not exist, most physicians will want to examine the ears after an episode of acute otitis media to be certain that the eardrums appear normal and the fluid has indeed disappeared from the middle ear.

*Chronic serous otitis media,* which may develop if the condition is not resolved, presents many problems. It may exist continually or fluctuate depending upon the degree of eustachian tube obstruction. Some days, perhaps when the student's nose is in its best condition, the eustachian tubes may work well. The slightest bit of added obstruction, however, may repeatedly bring about serous otitis.

A student with intermittent but almost constant eustachian tube problems may be sent to the physician by the clinician, who is certain that the child is not hearing well. By the time the child gets to the physician, the condition may have improved. The child is returned to school with assurances that all is well. A few weeks later the clinician is again perturbed about an obvious hearing loss. A trip to the physician again may result in an all-is-well diagnosis. This process can continue until the clinician and the physician are beginning to wonder about each other's qualifications! The only solution to this problem is communication. The clinician, the parents, and the physician must cooperate to have the student seen by the physician the same or following day of the suspected hearing loss.

If everything possible is done to relieve the eustachian tube obstruction and the serous otitis still persists, then surgical attention is directed to the middle ear itself. Again, this may take several forms. A simple *myringotomy,* lancing of the drum, may immediately allow air to gain entrance to the middle ear and may also allow the use of a very small tube to suck the fluid from the middle ear cavity. This simple myringotomy with aspiration may, in many cases, be sufficient to treat the serous otitis media. Often, however, this is not true and repeated myringotomies are needed.

The hole which is made in the eardrum at myringotomy would solve the problem if it stayed open. It would prevent the negative pressure from recurring in the middle ear. However, eardrums heal very well in most cases and repeated myringotomies are undesirable. As a result, a new procedure was developed within the last two decades which allows for ventilation of the middle ear space on a more permanent basis. This procedure consists of a myringotomy followed by the insertion of a tiny hollow polyethylene tube through the surgical perforation of the tympanic membrane, as illustrated in Figure 3-4. The tube is inserted after the fluid has been sucked from the ear.

The tube's purpose is not to drain the fluid from the ear but rather to prevent the recurrence of a vacuum in the ear by serving as an artificial eustachian tube.

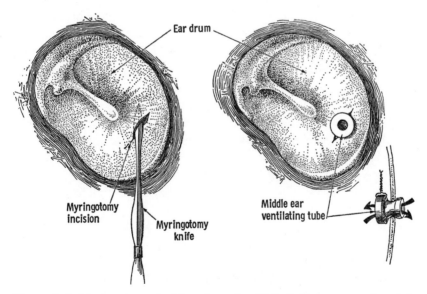

Figure 3-4. Myringotomy incision through which fluid is removed and in which a ventilating tube is placed.

Since polyethylene was the first material used for these tubes, the expression *P-E tube* was coined. More appropriately, they should be called ventilating tubes or artificial eustachian tubes. The main purpose of these tubes is to provide for ventilation of the middle ear space until the eustachian tube obstruction has been eliminated, or until normal growth and development lead to a better functioning eustachian tube.

The ventilating tubes are often allowed to remain in place for several years. However, the outer layer of the eardrum is skin, and skin grows and sheds. Thus, eardrum tissue moves, and often the tubes become dislodged with this migration of skin. If the serous otitis recurs after the tubes are extruded and the drum heals, it may be necessary to replace the tubes.

While the tubes are in place, the patient has a perforated eardrum with a tube sticking through it. Surprisingly enough, the hearing is often normal or near normal. Unfortunately, however, this man-made perforation is still a perforation. Therefore, the patient must take the usual precautions of keeping water out of the ear while swimming or bathing.

In summary, serous otitis media is the major enemy of normal hearing in the student. It is often difficult to diagnose. It is often difficult to treat. Most cases occur because there is something wrong with the eustachian tube's function. If the cause for the tubal problem can be identified and treated, then the serous otitis may well subside by itself. If no cause is found, or if all treatment of the suspected cause is unsuccessful, then the middle ear itself is approached through a surgical opening in the drum and the diseased contents evacuated. In order to insure continued ventilation of the middle ear, a tube is often placed through the drum, not to drain away the fluid, but to maintain adequate air exchange.

It is logical to ask what might happen to the ear if this fluid is not removed. Allowing fluid to remain is certainly not to be recommended. In most cases, the continual or recurring negative pressure may cause the eardrum to be further retracted into the middle ear space. This chronic condition can lead to a variety of serious ear problems which will not be covered in this discussion.

*Sensorineural Hearing Loss*

Sensorineural hearing loss, seen often in the school age child, usually proves to be a more perplexing problem than conductive hearing loss. This type of loss is due to a disease process in the inner ear structures and/or the auditory nerve and its pathways in the brain. Its etiologies are varied and often difficult to identify.

Sensorineural losses, like many other disease processes can be classified in a multitude of ways. For practical purposes, the author will consider hearing loss as either hereditary or acquired. Under the latter category, the acquired types will be considered to be either pre-natal, peri-natal, or post-natal.

It is convenient to be able to classify diseases and distinguish different types and their causes, but it often is not simple to do so. In almost half of the children seen with sensorineural hearing losses, the exact cause is never determined. Some of these may have been due to unrecognized mild infantile or childhood diseases. Undoubtedly, some are strictly hereditary.

HEREDITARY HEARING LOSS: There are many forms of hereditary hearing loss. These are all due to some defect in the genes transmitted from the parents. In many cases, the hearing loss may be the only defect. In many other cases, a syndrome, combination of conditions, may be present with poor hearing as one of the defects. Defects in the kidneys, or eyes, or other organs may also be present. There are a great number of these syndromes. They are often named after the individual who first noted and documented them. Fortunately, there are several symptoms or signs involved in the syndrome group, and they are usually diagnosed early.

ACQUIRED HEARING LOSS: Sensorineural hearing losses which are not the result of faulty genes, but rather are due to some disease condition which developed after the ovum was fertilized and the embryo came into existence, belong in the category of acquired hearing loss.

If this *pre-natal* category consists of those losses which came about while the child was being developed in the uterus, then these losses must be caused by something that happened to the mother.

Maternal rubella or German measles of the mother, probably accounts for most of the cases of children born with a sensori-neural hearing loss. The virus easily invades the uterus and the developing child. It does the most damage if the mother gets the disease during the first month of pregnancy, but it is dangerous at any time, especially during the first three months of pregnancy. Rubella is not the only virus which can cause deformities in the newborn. However, it is by far the most common. Perhaps some of the many cases of sensorineural hearing loss for which we can find no cause were actually due to a virus infection in the mother which was forgotten or not severe enough to be noted.

The toxemias of pregnancy also have been blamed for some cases of congenital deafness. These are diseases which have to do with kidney function and the regulation of blood pressure in pregnant women. The real cause is not known, and like most diseases, they can be quite mild or severe.

Jaundice of the newborn, erythroblastosis fetalis, or kernic-terus, may also cause hearing loss in the newborn. This disease may damage the nuclei, or centers of hearing, in the brain. It is due to an incompatibility of different factors of the two parents' blood types in the baby.

It appears that there are many situations which may develop in the pregnant woman which are potentially harmful to the baby. Close medical observation and supervision are important in minimizing this threat.

*The peri-natal* category has to do with the time immediately prior to and immediately after birth. It is sometimes not easy to accurately identify the exact time of damage to the hearing mechanism during this period, for the actual birth process may be as short as minutes, or as long as hours.

The peri-natal period is of importance when one considers the hearing losses which might occur during this time. For example, it is essential that the child receive adequate oxygen at all times. Hypoxia, or shortage of oxygen, brings about damage to delicate nerves in the brain. Also, if there is unusually great pressure on the head or the umbilical cord during labor and delivery, or if the child does not breathe well after being born, he may be affected by an oxygen shortage.

If the child is premature, his hearing apparatus may well be normal since it was formed very early during his development, but the child may be so small and weak that he cannot carry on the body functions needed to support all his normal body functions. Thus, damage may occur to the hearing mechanism.

Fortunately, the above described situations are not common. They are cited only to point out that the child's hearing can be in jeopardy from many causes, not only from the cradle-to-the-grave but before the cradle.

Infections in early childhood *(post-natal period)* may be of many types. The usual childhood diseases may be of the viral type such as chicken pox, measles (rubeola), German measles (rubella), or mumps. However, almost any severe viral disease, especially if it is with high fever, may harm the sensorineural mechanisms of hearing.

Bacterial infections also may produce hearing loss. They are different from viral infections in many complicated ways. To be very basic, one might say that viruses do not cause a large production of leukocytes or white blood cells, and as such, do not produce pus. Also, viruses often have affinity for directly attacking nervous tissue. Bacteria also may attack nervous tissue, but indirectly, by producing toxins that have an affinity for nerves, for example, typhoid or diphtheria. However, bacteria usually cause trouble by directly invading the structures. They may cause hearing loss by initiating an otitis which may invade the inner ear, or may cause a meningitis which subsequently damages the sensorineural hearing structures.

Drugs, although very beneficial, can also be potentially dangerous to the student's hearing. Some drugs, such as streptomycin, kanamycin, neomycin, and others are known to occasionally cause hearing loss. Why are they used? Most physicians are well aware of the dangers of many drugs. They are used sparingly, and only when the risk of not using them exceeds the risk of using them. Some infections respond only to these potentially ototoxic drugs.

Trauma can cause sensorineural hearing loss by several methods. A blow to the head may cause a skull fracture in the area of the temporal bone and injure any or all of the conducting mechanism, the cochlea, or the auditory nerve. Even a simple concussion, if severe enough, can do damage to the delicate sensorineural mechanism of hearing.

A more subtle but much more frequent type of trauma, noise, can also affect the hearing. Acoustic trauma can be in the form of a loud blast, which can damage the conducting mechanism of the middle ear. More frequently trauma may be of much lower intensity but prolonged or repetitive in nature. Many young students are exposing themselves almost daily to many damaging noise sources.

Medical and surgical advancements in the past years have been great, but they in themselves have also brought some additional health problems, both to the old and to the young. Many children are being born now who probably would not have survived even twenty years ago. Also, many children born with congenital defects are being saved. *Thus, in the coming years we are apt to see more multiple-handicapped students, many with sensorineural hearing loss.* Also the antibiotics prevent many cases of meningitis from developing, and they cure many cases which have developed, some of which, however, will have residual deficiencies such as hearing loss.

In conclusion, the clinician should not forget that students with sensorineural losses can also have the same illnesses as other students. They, too, can have otitis media. The otitis media can cause additional hearing loss. Thus, if any type of ear or hearing problem appears to further trouble the student with sensorineural loss, it should be promptly evaluated by a physician.

## SUMMARY

There are many medical implications related to the hearing-impaired student. In fact, after enumerating all the possible causes of decreased hearing, it is a wonder that most of us hear as well as we do. Adequate hearing plays such a major role in our language processes that we must constantly be on the alert to detect its impairment.

Certainly a student should have an examination of the ears, nose, and throat, including a good medical history and audiogram at the onset of his first year of school. It is most important to identify any hearing loss very early so that it can be classified as to degree and type, and appropriate medical therapy instituted.

# CHAPTER IV

# PSYCHOLOGICAL CONSIDERATIONS OF HARD OF HEARING CHILDREN

## Cornelius P. Goetzinger

WITH THE DEVELOPMENT of psychology as a science in this country, attention was focused on the effects of hearing impairment upon behavior. Several investigators, around the turn of the century, conducted studies comparing normal and hearing-impaired children on a number of mental tasks such as memory, word association, size and weight differences, etc. (Taylor, 1897; Mott, 1900; Smith, 1903; MacMillan and Bruner, 1906). However, it remained for Pintner and his associates (Pintner and Paterson, 1917; Pintner and Paterson, 1918; Pintner, Eisenson and Stanton, 1941) to develop the basic tools for quantitatively assessing the impact of auditory sensory deprivation upon human behavior. Despite their efforts and subsequent research, spanning more than a half century, there are many gaps in our knowledge, contingent not only upon the numerous facets of the problem still to be explored but also upon our incredibly changing times which have recast old as well as given rise to new dimensions for study. Therefore, the basic purpose of this chapter is to discuss the psychological concomitants of auditory impairment, as revealed by research and clinical experience, with special emphasis upon the hearing handicapped child attending the regular school.

## HISTORICAL PERSPECTIVE

The pure-tone audiometer was introduced commercially around 1922; but, it was not until after the Public Health survey of 1935-36 (Watson and Tolan, 1949; Davis and Silverman, 1960) that a standard zero reference for air conducted pure tones was developed in this country. An earlier attempt to utilize a threshold reference based on the laboratory minimal audible pressure curve of Sivian and White (Sivian and White, 1933) had resulted in an abnormally high incidence of hearing impairment in subjects who had been tested on audiometers calibrated to this reference (Watson and Tolan, 1949).

The Public Health survey data, or Beasley study, provided the data upon which American Standards Association (ASA) zero reference level for pure tones was subsequently based (ASA, Z24.5-1951). Figure 4-1 shows the 1951 (ASA) zero reference to which American pure-tone audiometers were calibrated, as well as the Sivian and White minimal audible pressure curve of 1933 and the new ISO (International Standards Organization) curve of 1964 (Davis, 1965). Also shown are the Beasley U. S. Public

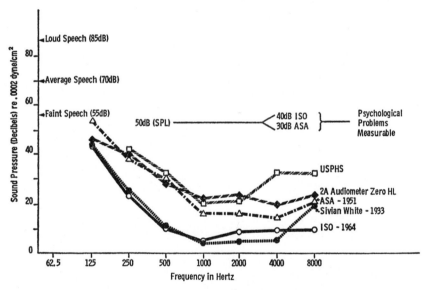

Figure 4-1. The figure presents a number of reference thresholds which may be encountered in the literature. As shown, the ISO 1964 reference threshold curve for pure tones with earphones is similar to the minimum audible pressure curve of Sivian and White of 1933. These references are more sensitive indices than the ASA earphone standard of 1951. For comparison, the Beasley USPH survey and the 2A audiometer zero references are shown. Other references include the levels of faint (fifty-five dB) average (seventy dB) and loud (eighty-five dB) speech and the pure-tone levels at which psychological problems are observable (thirty dB ASA or forty dB ISO).

Health Survey and the 2A Audiometer zero hearing level curves (Davis and Silverman, 1960).

It is obvious that the new ISO zero hearing level reference is similar to the minimal audible pressure curve of Sivian and White (1933). Furthermore, it can be seen that the ISO standard is a more severe zero reference than the ASA curve of 1951. However, it should be pointed out that American audiometers are now being calibrated to the American National Standards Institute norm (ANSI, 1969). This norm for the TDH-39 earphone is close to the ISO curve for the W.E. 705 earphone (ANSI, 1969).

As is noted in Figure 4-1, the hearing threshold level at which psychological problems become measurable is thirty dB (ASA) or forty dB (ISO). As will be pointed out in a subsequent section of this chapter, psychological research has indicated clearly that educational and emotional problems also begin to develop when hearing losses reach about a thirty dB (ASA) or a forty dB (ISO) level.

## VARIABLES RELATED TO HEARING IMPAIRMENT

Degree or amount of hearing loss is the variable most commonly associated with auditory impairment. The age at onset of deafness as well as the type of deafness also must be taken into account in evaluating the psychological impact of hearing loss.

### Degree of Hearing Loss

Degree of hearing loss is the fundamental variable related to auditory deficit. As indicated in Figure 4-1, when hearing loss approximates the thirty dB (ASA) or the forty dB (ISO) hearing level, psychological problems are measurable.

In order to assist the reader in understanding the relationship between the ASA and the ISO references, Table 4-I was prepared. The table presents several levels of hearing loss (average for five hundred, one thousand, and two thousand Hz in the better ear) in their relationship to (a) magnitude of handicap (as modified from Davis and Silverman, 1960, and NINDB reference, 1968); (b) speech understanding ability; (c) psychological impact; (d) need for hearing aid (modified from lectures by

TABLE 4-I

CLASSIFICATIONS BASED UPON HEARING HANDICAP

| Hearing Loss in dB† | | Handicap | Speech Understanding | Psychological Implications | Hearing Aid Need | Pittsburgh, Pa. Study of 4064 Subjects for C.A. 5-10 yrs. |
|---|---|---|---|---|---|---|
| ISO | ASA | | | | | |
| 0 | -10 | None | None when both ears are within this range. | None | None (The CROS with unilateral cases at times). | Number in class was 3996 (98.3 percent) |
| 25 | 15 | Slight | Difficulty only with faint speech. | Children may evince a slight verbal deficit. | Occasional use. | Number was 36 (0.9 percent) |
| 40 | 30 | Mild | Frequent trouble with normal speech at one meter (SPL of 65-70 dB). | Psychological problems are measurable in children. The beginning of social inadequacy in adults. | Hearing aids are often needed. | Number was 19 (0.5 percent) |
| 55 | 45 | Marked | Frequent difficulty with loud speech of about 85 dB SPL at one meter. | Children usually are retarded educationally if they are not given special help. Emotional and social problems are frequent. Psychological problems measurable in adults. | Generally, the area of greatest satisfaction from a hearing aid. | Number was 9 (0.2 percent) |
| 70 | 60 | Severe | Might understand shouted or amplified speech, but this will depend upon other factors as type of loss, etc. | Congenitally and prelingually deaf children usually show marked educational retardation. Emotional and social problems observable in children and adults. | In general, good results, but benefit is contingent upon many factors, as auditory discrimination. | Number given as 2 (0.05 percent) It includes the "extreme" class. |
| 90 | 80 | Extreme | Generally, no understanding of speech, even though amplified. | Congenitally and prelingually deaf may show severe educational retardation and emotional underdevelopment. Deafened adults may have personal and social problems. | Help from hearing aid depends on objectives. Lipreading, voice quality, etc. are often improved. | |

† A 10 rather than an 11 decibel difference for the average of the speech frequencies (500, 1000 and 2000 Hz) between the ISO and ASA references was used for convenience.

Dr. Raymond Carhart); and, finally, (e) relative to percent of public school children falling within each hearing level classification as determined in the Pittsburgh study* (NINDB, 1968).

Most of the psychological studies involving hearing loss in children in the regular schools were conducted prior to the advent of the ISO reference. Therefore, most studies used or appeared to have used a hearing threshold level reference approximating the ASA reference.

As may be observed in Table 4-I, the incidence of hearing loss for children five to ten years of age, in the Pittsburgh study, was seventeen in one thousand cases. Sixteen out of the aforementioned seventeen children per thousand had hearing deficits which ranged from slight through marked impairment (twenty-five to seventy dB ISO range). Therefore, it is with this segment of the hearing loss population with which this chapter will be primarily concerned.

### Age at Onset of Deafness

Age at onset of deafness is particularly important in connection with congenital and prelingual hearing impairment, as contrasted with adventitious deafness. Research (Reamer, 1921; Day, Fusfeld and Pintner, 1928) during the early decades of this century showed that children who were either congenitally deaf or had suffered severe deafness, prior to the ages four to six years, were retarded in later educational achievement as compared to children who became deaf after the aforementioned age range. Thus, the adventitiously (or postlingually) deaf children benefitted from having once heard. However, a chronological age of three years instead of four to six years is regarded now as the critical age of demarcation, primarily because of early diagnosis, parent and infant training programs, and preschools for the deaf. It is interesting, in this connection, that the findings from research in linguistics indicate that the basic elements of one's native language are mastered by ages three to four and one-half years (McNeill, 1965). Age of onset of hearing impair-

---

*The percentages in each classification as shown by the Pittsburgh study must be used with caution. They may not be universally applicable.

ment is therefore an important psychological aspect which influences the child's behavior.

### Type of Hearing Loss

Generally speaking, the deleterious effects of hearing impairment increase as the lesion progresses from the periphery inward. For example, the ability to discriminate and understand clearly the speech of another is usually normal in conductive impairment of the outer or middle ear. This is in contrast to inner ear deafness in which there is distortion of the heard speech to a greater or lesser extent. Moreover, the distortion is related to the degree of hearing loss and is generally more severe in retrocochlear lesions of the eighth nerve than in cochlear injury. Furthermore, the maximum conductive hearing loss of external or middle ear origin does not exceed sixty to seventy dB (ISO) in contrast to cochlear or retrocochlear deafness which may be total.

As will be observed in Table 4-I, the hard of hearing are classified as those who have a hearing level, in the better ear, within the twenty-five to seventy dB (ISO) range. When the hearing level in the better ear exceeds seventy dB (ISO), the classification is, in general, educational deafness (NINDB, 1968). However, there is no hard and fast demarcation between the hard of hearing and the educationally deaf as there are numerous variables (intelligence, background of the individual, age at onset, type of deafness, etc.) which may enter into such a classification. Generally, those with hearing losses of less than seventy dB (ISO) are more likely to have functional hearing than those with greater hearing loss.

### PSYCHOLOGICAL ASPECTS OF HARD OF HEARING CHILDREN

Research (Pintner and Lev, 1939) indicated that subjects with hearing losses between twenty-five to forty dB (ISO) were retarded about eight points on verbal, group tests of intelligence, even though they obtained an average IQ of one hundred on nonverbal group tests. Therefore, Pintner and Lev recommended that either nonverbal group tests or individual performance scales be utilized with hearing-impaired children.

The retardation on the verbal tests could be attributed either to poor reading skills or a slight language lag or a combination of both factors. Hence, the impact even of a slight hearing loss was measurable in the verbal area.

Research through the years has confirmed these earlier findings that hard of hearing children manifest a retardation, in verbal acquisition, and furthermore, that the inferiority is more apparent with increasing hearing loss (Pintner, Eisenson and Stanton, 1941; Young and McConnell, 1957). The findings do not imply that hard of hearing children are intellectually subnormal, but the findings do bring into focus the impact of hearing loss upon verbal growth and point up one area of educational need.

When hearing loss in the better ear is about forty dB (ISO) or greater, significant differences between hard of hearing and normally hearing children have been observed in adjustment and emotional maturity (Goetzinger, 1962; Goetzinger, Harrison and Baer, 1964; Fisher, 1966). The hard of hearing tend to have more emotional problems, which may be apparent either by withdrawal tendencies, overaggressiveness, or a combination of both. There is also some evidence that hearing-impaired children are not accepted as well by classmates as the normally hearing (Elser, 1959).

Age at onset and type of hearing loss are important variables in assessing psychological implications. Research indicates that congenital, sensorineural deafness of about forty dB (ISO) induces a retardation in language development of one to one-and-one-half years at a chronological age of three (Goetzinger, 1962; Goetzinger, Harrison and Baer, 1964). In other words, a child of about three to three-and-one-half years of age will be at a two to two-and-one-half year level in language development even though his intelligence on performance scales is normal. Furthermore, auditory discrimination is reduced but essentially improves with training and age. The reduced initial auditory discrimination, in such cases, reflects the language lag.

An implication of these findings, in addition to the need for early training, pertains to diagnosis. More specifically, *young hearing-impaired children who show language delay are not infrequently diagnosed as retarded or aphasic.* The latter diagnosis is often predicated on the observation of a telegraphic-like language pattern, contingent upon good hearing in the lower frequencies (a sloping audiogram). Better hearing sensitivity in the low frequencies permits the child to respond to the low frequency components of speech and environmental sounds. This gives the impression that he has normal hearing throughout the *entire* frequency range, which he does not. The important point is that the diagnostician (particularly psychologists) should first obtain information on the child's hearing sensitivity before administering tests and arriving at a diagnosis.

### Slight-to-Moderate Hearing Loss

As noted previously, the majority of five to ten year old children with hearing losses in the Pittsburgh study fell within the twenty-five to seventy dB (ISO) hearing loss range, Table 4-I. Furthermore, 1.4 percent of the total with hearing loss were found in the slight and mild hearing loss classifications, i.e. 0.9 percent in the twenty-five to forty dB (ISO) range and 0.5 percent in the forty to fifty-five dB (ISO) range.

Past research has indicated that slight and mild hearing impairments may induce psychological problems in children. Yet, these children are most amenable to help, particularly in view of early diagnosis and with respect to the areas of need (language, school achievement, emotional problems, etc.). In general, excluding severe learning problems, these children will progress satisfactorily in the regular classroom with a minimum of remediation. Conversely, if the hearing loss exceeds fifty-five dB (ISO) there is likelihood that special classes for the hard of hearing may be required. However, it will be dependent upon a number of factors such as type of hearing loss, age at onset, intelligence, age at diagnosis, extent of training, remediation provided, use of prosthesis (hearing aid), etc.

Young and McConnell (1957), in a well controlled study, compared hard of hearing and normal hearing children in vocabulary (equating them for age, race, sex, socio-economic status and nonverbal intelligence). The mean hearing loss in the better ear of the hard of hearing children was sixty-one dB (ISO) which is indicative of marked deafness.

The results showed the normals to be superior to the hard of hearing in vocabulary. In fact, no hard of hearing subject exceeded his matched control on the test. In addition, every hard of hearing child showed verbal retardation when considered in terms of his intellectual potential, as measured with the nonverbal Raven's Progressive Matrices Test.

### Marked Hearing Loss

As indicated in Table 4-I, the incidence of children with marked hearing loss of fifty-five to seventy dB (ISO) was about 0.2 percent (two out of one thousand). Children with this degree of deficit in the better ear, particularly if the impairment obtains from birth and is sensorineural, will have difficulty both educationally and psychologically in the ordinary classroom. This is true unless they have considerable additional help in school work from a special teacher and the home. As previously mentioned, some may require attendance in a special classroom for the hard of hearing.

Unfortunately, educators are not well acquainted with the impact of deafness upon educational achievement, language acquisition, and emotional adjustment. They are, therefore, inclined to ascribe nothing less than miraculous powers to speechreading and hearing aids. They seem to think that a child's problems are resolved after being fitted with a hearing aid in conjunction with a few lipreading lessons. However, nothing could be further from the truth, not unless educational retardation and emotional problems are regarded as acceptable goals in such cases.

### Severe and Extensive Hearing Loss

As may be seen in Table 4-I, the number of children with severe and extensive hearing losses is only one out of a thousand. Pintner and Lev (1939), in an extensive study of hard of hearing children in the New York City school system, reported none with hearing loss greater than about fifty-five dB (ISO) in the better ear (an analysis of their graph). Apparently, children at that time with severe and extreme hearing losses were educated in schools and classes for the deaf.

With reference to the deaf, there is an extensive literature over a period of more than sixty years which deals with their educational and psychological problems (Goetzinger, 1972).

## LEARNING IN HEARING-IMPAIRED CHILDREN

One of the most significant series of studies pertaining to learning in normal and hearing-impaired children has recently been completed by Gaeth (1967). Using a paired-associates paradigm, he investigated the efficacy of unimodal and bimodal methods of presenting material to be learned. The three methods of learning under study were visual, auditory and audio-visual. For normal hearing children, significant differences were not found among the three methods for paired-associate word lists. For the hard of hearing within the twenty-six to forty, forty-one to fifty-five, and fifty-six to seventy dB (ISO) hearing loss classifications, there were nonsignificant differences between the visual and the bimodal audio-visual methods. However, both of the aforementioned were superior to the auditory approach. With reference to the results Gaeth (1967) stated, ". . . it argues for revisions in the educational management of hard of hearing children" (p. 282).

When the three methods were compared for children in the seventy-one to eighty-one dB (ISO) hearing loss range, the purely visual approach was superior to the audio-visual as well as to the auditory approach. Gaeth (1967) reasoned that ". . . the material was not very intelligible and either confused the task somewhat or distracted the children from functioning as efficiently as they did visually" (p. 284).

As simple material, reasonably well known to the subjects had been used in the foregoing experiments, it was decided to repeat them with new materials, hypothesizing that the bimodal presentation is critical when either the normal or the hard of hearing child is learning new words and concepts. In these new experiments nonverbal and nonmeaningful symbols, nonsense syllables, and simple meaningful sounds were utilized in various combinations. As a result of a variety of experiments Gaeth concluded that originally the child learns either in one or the other channel (visual or auditory) but not in both channels simultaneously. Furthermore, the child selects the channel with the more meaningful material. Finally, with reference to the child with extreme hearing loss Gaeth (1967) wrote:

> Interestingly the same conglomeration of experiments presented to deaf children suggest that the preceding statement must be reinterpreted, since with them the predominance of performance in the visual modality is so strong it tends to override the more usual definition of meaningfulness. Finally, our current inference is that when individuals do show benefit from a bimodal presentation, such as in the apparent combination of lipreading and hearing through a hearing aid, it is being done, not from the integration of simultaneous bimodal presentation, but the integration of rapidly alternating unimodal stimulation. It would appear that these data have implications for the educational management of the hard of hearing and deaf child (p. 292).

Gaeth's reference to bimodal improvement for lipreading and hearing through a hearing aid is amply supported by the research findings of Hudgins (1951), Prall (1957), Kelly (1967), Purcell and Costello (1970) and Sanders (1971). More explicitly, the aforementioned investigators have demonstrated that a bimodal presentation, as discussed, is significantly superior to a unimodal visual presentation for hearing-imparied children.

What then is the reason for the differences between Gaeth's findings and the research results reported for lipreading, hearing, and amplification? Briefly, Gaeth's visual presentations consisted of words, nonsense syllables, and nonsense symbols presented in printed form as in reading. The other researchers used lipreading for the visual input which is an entirely different form. The former (visual printed form) is a precise and stable technique for the transmission of information as compared to lipreading which is characteristically an imprecise medium. Purcell and Costello (1970) called attention to these differences earlier.

The hard of hearing usually experience an auditory discrimination loss of greater or lesser degree, so that, in essence, they are processing two distorted inputs during bimodal reception involving lipreading, hearing, and hearing aids. In this instance the two distorted inputs, simultaneously processed, appear to interact to produce additional cues so that the bimodal presentation is superior either to the visual (lipreading) or auditory (hearing) alone.

In Gaeth's experiments the conditions were different for the hard of hearing. Briefly, his visual modality (the printed form) represents a highly precise and clear medium for the conveyance of thought as compared to lipreading. In fact, reception through vision, using this medium, should be superior to the auditory, primarily because of the auditory discrimination loss or distortion associated frequently with hearing impairment (principally, cochlear and retrocochlear). Hence, Gaeth found, as would be expected, not only superiority of the visual over the auditory modality, but in addition, the unimodal visual equal to and in some instances, superior to the bimodal (visual-auditory) presentation.

In connection with the foregoing discussion was the research conducted recently at the National Technical Institute for the Deaf (NTID) which pertained to the relative efficacy of lipreading, the sign language and printed material in conveying meaning to deaf students. (Stuckless, 1971, reporting on the study of Robert Gates of NTID). Gates selected one hundred forty subjects in the beginning class at NTID and randomly assigned them to seven groups of twenty each. Criteria for selection were the absence of any serious visual defects and at least an eighth grade reading ability. Each group was presented with the same 2000 word test passage, under seven different presentation conditions, utilizing video tape and split screen technique. All presentations were at a rate of 125 words per minute. A thirty-nine item multiple choice test was devised to test their comprehension. The seven presentations were: (1) spoken without sound, i.e., lipreading; (2) manual communication only; (3) the printed form of the lecture; (4) a combination of the spoken and signed lecture; (5) a combination of the spoken and printed lecture; (6) a combination of the signed and printed lecture; and (7) a combination of the spoken, signed, and printed lecture. The results are seen in Table 4-II.

Several of the findings are of more than passing interest in the context of this discussion. First, the spoken (lipreading, i.e. *L.R.*) and the sign language give equally poor results (see Table 4-II). Both are imprecise vehicles, carrying relatively high levels of distortion. Combining the two, resulting in a mean score of 13.7, does not increase intelligibility. In short, simultaneous reception through the visual modality of two distorted presentations does not improve understanding as is the case when distorted visual and auditory signals are receptively processed. However, there is a significant increase in the mean score (26.05) when the printed symbol is used. Also seen in Table 4-II, the mean score remains virtually that of the printed symbol when the aforementioned is combined either with the sign language (mean score, 23.95) or with lipreading (mean score, 25.75). Furthermore, combining the three modes of transmission does not improve reception over the printed symbol alone, Table 4-II.

These findings indicate that neither the sign language, lipreading, nor a combination of the two are as effective as the printed word for conveying information. In addition, combining the sign language, lipreading and the printed word does not improve reception over the printed word alone. Apparently, the organism can attend only to one visual presentation mode. That mode is

TABLE 4-II

RESULTS OF NTID STUDY

| Method of Presentation | Mean Score | Standard Deviation |
|---|---|---|
| 1. Spoken (lipreading) only | 13.50 | 3.73 |
| 2. Manual (seeing) only | 15.05 | 3.87 |
| 3. Printed symbol (graphic or reading) only | 26.05 | 7.70 |
| 4. Spoken (L.R.) and signs combined | 13.70 | 2.43 |
| 5. Spoken (L.R.) and graphic (reading) combined | 25.65 | 7.36 |
| 6. Sign and graphic (reading) combined | 23.95 | 6.87 |
| 7. Spoken (L.R.), signed and graphic (reading) combined | 25.65 | 10.05 |

used which provides the maximum in information. Reading, in this case being the most precise and stable one, is utilized.

With reference to the hard of hearing in the seventy-one to eighty-five dB (ISO) range, as well as the deaf, Gaeth (1967) demonstrated the superiority of the visual over the combined auditory-visual modes when the former (visual) was the printed word. In short, adding severely distorted auditory signals to clear visual signals reduced information. However, when the visual mode is lipreading, the combined visual-auditory approach is superior (Hudgins, 1951; Sanders, 1971).

Irrespective of the superiority of the auditory-visual mode over either one alone, when lipreading is the visual mode, it is unlikely that the aforementioned either would equal or excel the visual modality when the printed symbol is used (e.g. Gaeth and Gates). This brings up the question of utilizing a more precise lipreading method such as cued speech in conjunction with auditory amplification to improve reception during communication. In short, there is need for research in this area. However, the use of so-called simultaneous methods (i.e., using either the sign language, the manual alphabet or both in conjunction with lipreading, hearing, and auditory amplification) would not be any more effective than the bimodal visual-auditory consisting of lipreading, hearing, and amplification. In addition, the latter combination in conjunction with cued speech might prove significantly superior to the simultaneous methods.

## SUMMARY

In summarizing this section on hearing loss of children in the regular schools, the following points appear to be noteworthy:

1. Children with hearing levels in the better ear which lie within the zero to twenty-five dB (ISO) range do not manifest psychological atypicalness either in verbal intelligence or in adjustment.
2. Children within the twenty-five to forty dB (ISO) range in the better ear, are likely to show significant retardation on verbal tests of intelligence, but will still test within the nor-

mal range (IQ ninety to one hundred ten). A retardation in verbal intelligence will probably reflect the language lag contingent upon the slight hearing loss.

3. Children with hearing losses of about forty dB (ISO) in the better ear frequently show retardation in educational achievement and deviation from normal in emotional and social adjustment. These children will need help in compensating for their hearing loss.

4. Congenital sensorineural hearing losses of about forty dB (ISO) in the better ear appear to induce a language lag of twelve to eighteen months at age three years. Auditory discrimination, although poor at this age level because of the hearing deficit, eventually reaches a satisfactory level with increasing age. At age three such children are not infrequently diagnosed as aphasic, learning disability cases, brain damaged, etc.

5. Children with slight hearing losses, twenty-five to forty dB (ISO) in the better ear, will at times require hearing aids and frequently auditory amplification.

6. Children with hearing losses of forty dB (ISO) or greater, in the better ear, generally require the use of amplification and hearing aids. These children should do well in the regular schools with proper help.

7. Children with hearing losses of fifty-five to seventy dB (ISO), in the better ear, may require education in the special classes for the hard of hearing in the schools.

8. When hearing losses in the better ear exceed seventy dB (ISO), the general classification is educational deafness. Such children are usually educated either in private or public residential schools for the deaf, or in special classes for the severe hearing loss cases in the regular schools. Finally, all recommendations relative to the use of hearing aids and auditory amplification imply that corrective surgery was contraindicated.

## REFERENCES

American National Standards Institute. ANSI Specifications for Audiometers. New York, ANSI, (S3.6-1969), 1969.

American Standards Association. Audiometers for General Diagnostic Purposes. New York, ASA Bulletin (Z24.5-1951), 1951.

Davis, H.: Guide for the classification and evaluation of hearing handicap in relation to the International Audiometric Zero. *Transactions of the American Academy of Ophthalmology and Otolaryngology, 69*:740-751, 1965.

Davis, H. and Silverman, S. R.: *Hearing and Deafness.* New York, Holt, Rinehart and Winston, 1960.

Day, H. E., Fusfeld, I. S., and Pintner, R.: *A Survey of American Schools for the Deaf.* Washington, D. C., The National Research Council, 1928.

Elser, R. P.: The social position of hearing handicapped children in the regular grades. *Except Children, 25*:305-309, 1959.

Fisher, B.: The social and emotional adjustment of children with impaired hearing attending ordinary classes. *Brit J Educ Psychol, 36*:319-321, 1966.

Gaeth, J. H.: Learning with visual and audio-visual presentations. In McConnell, F., and Ward, P. H. (Eds.): *Deafness in Childhood.* Nashville, Vanderbilt University Press, 1967, pp. 279-303.

Goetzinger, C. P.: The psychology of hearing impairment. In Katz, J. (Ed.): *Handbook of Clinical Audiology.* Baltimore, Williams & Wilkins, 1972, pp. 666-693.

Goetzinger, C. P.: Effects of small perceptive losses on language and on speech discrimination. *Volta Rev, 64*:408-414, 1962.

Goetzinger, C. P., Harrison, C. and Baer, C. J.: Small perceptive hearing loss: its effects in school-age children. *Volta Rev, 66*:124-131, 1964.

Hudgins, C. V.: Problems of speech comprehension in deaf children. *Nervous Child, 9*, 1951.

Kelly, J. C.: *Audio-Visual Reading: A Manual for Training the Hard of Hearing in Voice Communication.* Urbana, University of Illinois Speech and Hearing Clinic, 1967.

MacMillan, D. P. and Bruner, F. G.: *Experimental studies of deaf children.* Special report of the department of child study and pedagogical investigation. Chicago, Chicago Public Schools, 1906.

McNeill, D.: The capacity for language acquisition. In *Research on Behavioral Aspects of Deafness.* U. S. Dept. of H.E.W., Washington, D. C., Vocational Rehabilitation Administration, 1965, pp. 11-28.

Mott, A. J.: A comparison of deaf and hearing children in their ninth year. *Amer Ann Deaf, 44*:401-412, 1899, and *45*:33-39, 1900.

NINDB Monograph No. 7. *Human Communication: The Public Health Aspects of Hearing, Language, and Speech Disorders.* U. S. Dept. of H.E.W., Bethesda, NINDB, 1968.

Pintner, R., and Lev, J.: The intelligence of the hard of hearing school child. *J Genet Psychol, 55*:31-48, 1939.

Pintner, R., and Paterson, D. G.: *A Scale of Performance.* New York, Appleton, 1917.

Pintner, R., and Paterson, D. G.: Some conclusions from psychological tests of the deaf. *Volta Rev, 20:*10-14, 1918.

Pintner, R., Eisenson, J., and Stanton, M.: *The Psychology of the Physically Handicapped.* New York, Crofts, 1941.

Prall, J.: Lipreading and hearing aids combine for better comprehension. *Volta Rev, 59:*64-65, 1957.

Purcell, G. and Costello, M. R.: Multisensory stimulation and verbal learning. *Bulletin of American Organization for the Education of the Hearing-Impaired (A. G. Bell Assoc for the Deaf)* 1:66-68, 1970.

Reamer, J. C.: Mental and psychological measurements of the deaf. *Psychological Monographs, No. 132.* Princeton, The Psychological Review, 1921.

Sanders, D. A.: *Aural Rehabilitation.* Englewood Cliffs, Prentice-Hall, 1971.

Sivian, L. J., and White, S. D.: On minimum audible sound fields. *J Acoust Soc Amer,* 4:288-321, 1933.

Smith, J. L.: Mental characteristics of pupils. *Amer Ann Deaf,* 48:248-268, 1903.

Stuckless, E. R.: Assessing and supporting linguistic development in deaf adolescents. (A lecture presented at the Hearing and Speech Conference at KUMC, Feb., 1971.) *KUMC Postgraduate Medical Study Handout,* 1971, pp. 7-13.

Taylor, H.: A spelling test. *Amer Ann Deaf,* 42:364-369, 1897.

Watson, L. A., and Tolan, T.: *Hearing Tests and Hearing Instruments.* Baltimore, Williams and Wilkins, 1949.

Young, C., and McConnell, F.: Retardation of vocabulary development in hard of hearing children. *Except Children,* 23:368-370, 1957.

# CHAPTER V

# SPEECH PROBLEMS AND SPEECH CORRECTION FOR THE HEARING-IMPAIRED CHILD

## JANE B. SEATON

THIS CHAPTER will present a discussion of the influence of hearing impairment on *speech,* as opposed to *language.* Speech can be very simply defined as the production of an oral (vocal) response. Classically, this includes *articulation* (position and movement of the lips, teeth, tongue and palate), *voice* (resonance), and *rhythm* (rate of utterance).

The speech problems discussed will be those encountered by the hearing-impaired child who has enough residual hearing to use the auditory channel successfully in a regular classroom. It will also be assumed that this child has developed speech and language prior to entering school and uses oral language as his primary means of communication.

A large portion of this chapter proposes a framework of information which can be used by the clinician in evaluating the speech of the hearing-impaired child. Acoustic factors, audiologic data, and the results of the clinician's speech and language evaluation will be presented as necessary and interrelated information basic to the therapy design.

Finally, the therapy setting, itself, will be discussed. The close interrelationship between speech and language and its effect on therapy goals and procedures for the hearing-impaired child will be explored. Suggestions will be given for designing appropriate therapy goals in order to make maximum use of available therapy time.

## PREDICTING AND IDENTIFYING SPEECH ERRORS

*Background Information*

Studies are available describing the speech characteristics of the deaf population, but there is limited research data available concerning the frequency and type of articulatory errors exhibited by those with a reasonable amount of residual hearing. Carhart (Davis and Silverman, 1960) has stated that a child in the latter category has different requirements for speech training than a child who is deaf. This statement is not followed by an elaboration of the specific errors that require correction or related methods for speech training.

Anderson (1953) was more specific when he described the speech sounds most likely to deteriorate as a result of hearing impairment. He felt that errors occur most frequently for sounds of high frequency and low phonetic power, sounds requiring the most complex adjustments of the articulators, and sounds least visible when produced.

Newby (1964) also stated that hearing loss would most likely affect the production of those sounds which are less visible, those that are more complex in formation (requiring precise adjustment of tongue tip or blade), and those with important high frequency characteristics. He noted that the two sounds most commonly affected by hearing impairment are /s/ and /r/. The writer's experience would tend to support this observation of /s/ and /r/ errors, however, documented information is not available regarding the frequency of misarticulated /s/ and /r/, or the type of misarticulations that are made by hearing-impaired individuals.

As the preceding review of literature implies, the clinician does have a few pieces of information from which he can predict the articulation errors which may occur as the result of hearing impairment. Fundamental knowledge of normal speech and language development, as well as information concerning the visual and acoustic properties of each phonetic unit, is necessary for error prediction, accurate error identification, and decisions concerning remediation.

For example, the hearing-impaired child usually exhibits de-/ layed development in speech, as well as in language. From this knowledge, one might predict that a certain portion of the omissions and substitutions observed are in a transitional state and may be self-corrected by the child or require only minimal instruction and reinforcement by the clinician. When a five-year-old child says *Me fum huht* instead of *My thumb hurts*, the clinician would be realistic in describing the articulation errors as developmental. The use of pronouns, in this example, is immature (*me* for *my*), and the omission of final /s/ in the word *hurts* is probably a verb agreement error, rather than an articulatory omission. Therefore, the /f/ for /th/ substitution in the word *thumb* is consistent with the immature language level of the utterance.

The hearing-impaired child usually exhibits a high depen-/ dence on visual cues. Thus, the bilabial /p/, /b/, and /m/, labio-dental /f/ and /v/, and lingual-dental voiced and voiceless /th/ consonant sounds are learned more easily by some children because they are easier to see. The hearing-impaired child will be more likely to have difficulty with these sounds if he is not attentive to visual cues. Obviously, the clinician will want to emphasize the visual aspects during attempts to stimulate correct production of these sounds.

*Acoustic Information*

Knowledge of the acoustic properties of phonetic units has important implications for predicting the articulation errors which may occur as a result of hearing impairment. This acoustic information is also useful for predicting the benefit to be derived from auditory stimulation for the correction of phonemes in error. In order to have appropriate expectations concerning the hearing-impaired child's speech errors and possible avenues of remediation for these errors, the clinician should be aware of the three major auditory cues by which phonetic units are detected (i.e. frequency, intensity, and duration) and the fact that the phonetic environment can also influence the audibility of phonemes.

FREQUENCY: If the frequency components of a specific sound are centered in a frequency range where the child has little or no hearing, production of this sound will most likely be defective unless he can learn to make maximum use of cues which make this phoneme distinct from all other phonetic units.

Vowels and nasal consonants have been shown to have the lowest frequency composition of all phonetic units. This could account for the lack of vowel distortion observed in the speech of a child whose hearing is normal below one thousand Hz. Frequently, the clinician will note excessive nasality in the speech of the hearing-impaired child. Possibly this is due to the low-frequency auditory feedback provided by the low-frequency nasality factor.

Voiceless continuants (/s/, /sh/, /f/, /th/, and /h/) have the highest frequency components of all phonetic units and are the most difficult to detect from auditory cues alone. Although /f/ and /th/ have high visibility, one could predict that these two phonemes are just as likely to be in error as the phonemes /s/, /sh/, and /h/ if the child is not attentive to visual cues.

INTENSITY: Intensity must be considered by the clinician in deciding if a sound can be made loud enough for the child to hear. Exploration of intensity has revealed that vowels are generally the loudest phonetic units, and voiced consonants are higher in intensity than their voiceless counterparts. Since most words contain several phonetic units with varying degrees of intensity, the sounds with low intensity are frequently not heard. For example, a child with a moderate hearing loss across the entire frequency range may hear vowels clearly but be unable to hear voiceless consonants in some contexts (e.g. *soap* could be heard as *oh*).

DURATION: The longer a sound is present, the easier it becomes to identify and compare with other sounds. However, duration alone usually does not provide enough information for accurate sound identification by the hearing-impaired child.

Vowels are generally of longer duration than consonants, with the exception of sibilant and fricative units (continuants). Voiceless sibilant and fricative units are also high-frequency and low-intensity units, which implies that the duration factor may not provide enough acoustic information for accurate identification by the hearing-impaired child. For example, although /s/ and /sh/ have longer duration than /d/ and /g/, the latter two units will be more easily detected by most hearing-impaired children because of the lower frequency and greater intensity of the latter two sounds.

PHONETIC ENVIRONMENT: The clinician should also be aware that frequency and temporal characteristics vary as a function of the phonetic environment of each unit. This may lead to the error inconsistency repeatedly observed when one listens to the hearing-impaired child. Although each phoneme has frequency, intensity, and duration that can be measured in isolation, these measurements will change when the phoneme is produced in conjunction with other phonemes. For example, if the child produces *take* for *cake,* but correctly produces *cow,* the cues have been sufficient for him to identify the /k/ in the phonetic environment of *cow* but not sufficient in the environment of *cake.*

SUMMARY: Acoustic information tells the clinician to check the frequency (how high), intensity (how faint), and duration (how short) for the phoneme in error. In addition, the phonetic environment in which the error occurred must be examined. The clinician must help the child make maximum use of any or all of the acoustic cues that are available and use supplementary visual and tactile cues when auditory stimulation is insufficient.

### Audiologic Information

It has been stated that the acoustic information presented in the preceding section can lead to error predictions for the hearing-impaired child. These predictions, however, will vary with the type, severity, and configuration of the child's hearing loss. This variation indicates the need for definitive audiologic results for every hearing-impaired child. Unfortunately, such results have not been routinely demanded by clinicians. An unpublished survey of twenty-three clinicians, conducted by the author, revealed a total of seventy-nine hearing-impaired children on their collective caseload. These same clinicians reported that they had not seen results of audiologic evaluations on thirty-five percent of these children.

Audiologic information can be useful to the clinician in terms of predicting speech errors and of probable benefit to be derived from various therapy techniques. For this reason, a complete audiologic work-up should be included in the diagnostic information obtained for each hearing-impaired child. This position can be best supported by the following example:

> S. C. had been receiving speech therapy in the public school for several years. The child's mother reported initial omission of sibilant sounds, but the author's evaluation revealed multiple distortions, with incorrect tongue movement being used in an attempt to compensate for the errors. Severe language problems were also noted. A hearing aid had been recommended by a local physician, but the child had resisted wearing it for some time. No significant improvement in speech was obtained while amplification was used. When S. C. finally did receive a complete audiological evaluation at eleven years of age, the results indicated normal hearing for the lower frequencies and a sharply dropping loss above five hundred Hz for both ears (Figure 5-1).

If this audiogram had been available to the clinician when the child was initially enrolled for therapy, the clinician could have predicted that the sibilant sounds would not be available to this child through the auditory channel because of the severe high-frequency loss. Difficulty tolerating amplification would have been predicted from the normal hearing in the low frequencies. Acoustic cues necessary for the refinement of high-frequency sounds in error would probably not be provided by conventional amplification due to the sharply dropping configuration of the loss.

All of the above described information would have initially led to more realistic and appropriate therapy goals and procedures if it had been available to the clinician when he first saw the child. More specifically, therapy should have emphasized maximum use of residual hearing, without amplification, combined with training in the use of visual cues. Certainly, refined production of sibilant sounds such as /s/ and /sh/ would not have been chosen as an initial therapy goal. These sounds would

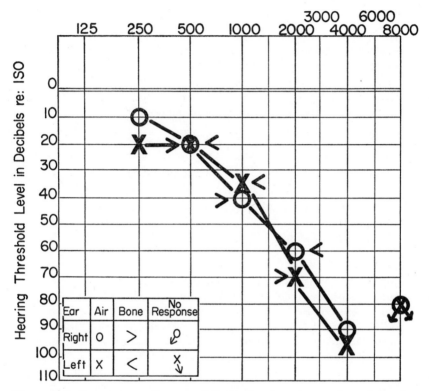

Figure 5-1. Pure tone audiogram of S. C. showing a sensorineural hearing loss which drops sharply above five hundred Hz.

be the most difficult for the child to master because the high frequency loss would not permit her to hear and monitor these sounds.

While each child must be evaluated as an individual, a few general guidelines concerning error-prediction from the severity, configuration, and type of loss can be given by a discussion of four broad categories of hearing loss as follows: (a) unilateral, (b) conductive, (c) high-frequency sensorineural, and (d) mild-to-moderate sensorineural. The loss of a severe-to-profound degree is not included, since full-time placement in a regular school setting usually is not appropriate for children with this amount of hearing loss.

UNILATERAL LOSS: The following case describes a child with a hearing loss in one ear only:

> H. S. failed his school hearing screening test at the end of first grade. Speech and language development were reported within normal limits. A follow-up audiologic evaluation revealed normal hearing for the right ear and a profound sensorineural hearing loss for the left ear. No articulation errors were present, and preferential seating in the classroom was the only recommendation.

As illustrated by the above case history, a hearing loss in one ear, even if severe, does not significantly interfere with speech development. Thus, if a child with a unilateral hearing loss has articulatory errors, these errors should not be attributed to the hearing loss. Other causal factors should be explored.

CONDUCTIVE LOSS: An example of a child with a conductive hearing loss is described below:

> S. D. was referred at thirteen years of age by the school after failing numerous hearing tests. Parents reported a long history of ear problems and hearing difficulty since she was a small child. Articulation was observed to be normal at the time of evaluation, but the parents' report indicated that speech and language development had been slow. Audiologic evaluation revealed a moderate air conduction hearing loss and normal hearing by bone conduction for both ears (Figure 5-2). S. D. is currently receiving medical treatment for severe ear infections. Preferential seating in the classroom has been recommended until the hearing problem is resolved.

The effect of a conductive hearing loss on speech production will vary with the age of onset and with the degree of loss. Mild conductive losses usually do not significantly affect articulation, regardless of when they occur. If the conductive loss is congenital, significant speech and language delay may occur, with resulting developmental articulation errors. If the loss is acquired after speech and language have developed, the child will usually exhibit no directly related articulation errors. If the loss is progressive, there may be a deterioration in speech after several months. Articulation, in the presence of progressive conductive

# PURE TONE AUDIOGRAM
## Frequency in Hertz

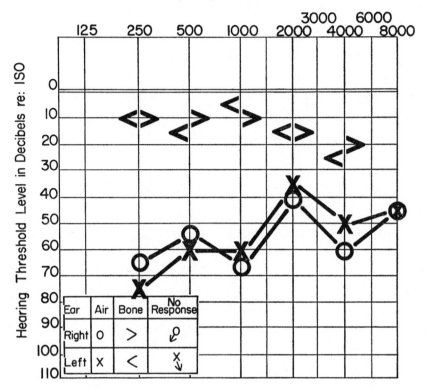

Figure 5-2. Pure tone audiogram of S. D. showing a moderate, bilateral conductive hearing loss.

hearing loss, will be less precise, and phonemes will become indistinct.

Very frequently, conductive hearing loss in children will fluctuate. These changes are usually related to the presence of active ear infections, and no related articulation errors occur. Vocal quality may be hyponasal if the nasal passages are blocked, but quality usually improves when the blockage is eliminated.

Frequently, one hears that conductive hearing loss results in lowered vocal intensity when a person with this type of loss speaks. The writer believes that this conclusion is not supported by enough statistical evidence to warrant its use as a predictive factor. Occasionally, the child with a significant conductive loss will have difficulty monitoring both his vocal pitch and intensity. His speech may be monotonous, and he may not increase the loudness of his speech appropriately to overcome a noisy environment.

All children with conductive hearing losses should receive a thorough medical examination to see if medical or surgical treatment will eliminate the hearing loss. If the conductive loss is not correctable, the child may receive considerable benefit from am-

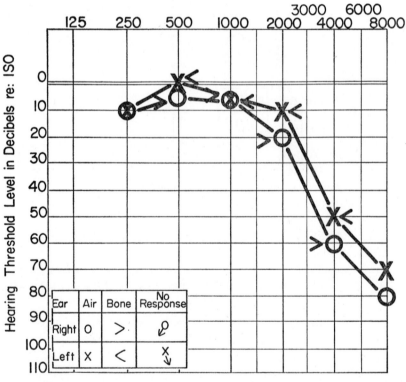

Figure 5-3. Pure tone audiogram of H. W. showing a bilateral, high-frequency sensorineural hearing loss above two thousand Hz.

plification, with resulting improvement in speech. As the child learns to use the auditory cues which become available to him through a hearing aid, auditory training provided by the clinician should increase the rate of speech improvement.

HIGH-FREQUENCY SENSORINEURAL LOSS: A child with a high-frequenty hearing loss *may* exhibit difficulty with voiceless continuants, but related articulation problems usually do not occur if the loss is above two thousand Hz. Normal hearing from two hundred fifty Hz through two thousand Hz is adequate for receiving the acoustic cues for all English phonetic units, as illustrated by the following case:

> H. W. was referred after failing his school hearing screening test at the beginning of first grade. Audiologic evaluation revealed a sensorineural loss above two thousand Hz for both ears (Figure 5-3). Speech evaluation revealed normal articulation of all phonemes and occasional difficulty with blends. The latter was considered within normal limits for the child's chronological age and not the result of the high-frequency hearing loss.

Children with high-frequency losses, above one thousand Hz are more likely to exhibit articulation errors related to their hearing impairment. The following case is an example of this type of hearing loss:

> C. W.'s hearing was found to be normal below one thousand Hz, a mild loss was present at one thousand Hz, and a severe loss was shown for the higher frequencies (Figure 5-4). His speech was easily understood, although multiple errors were present. Analysis of these errors revealed sound substitutions which appeared related to general developmental delay, documented by prior history and evaluation. However, omission of sibilant sounds was consistent and considered directly related to the hearing loss for higher frequency sounds.

The speech of a child with a high-frequency hearing loss will vary with his attention to visual cues. He frequently has enough residual hearing to supplement the visual channel to achieve correct production of nearly all phonetic units. The clinician should pay particular attention to the type and consistency of errors which occur in these cases. As stated previously, in the instance of a child with a high-frequency hearing loss, voiceless sibilants ( /s/ and /sh/ ) are most likely to be affected, and the er-

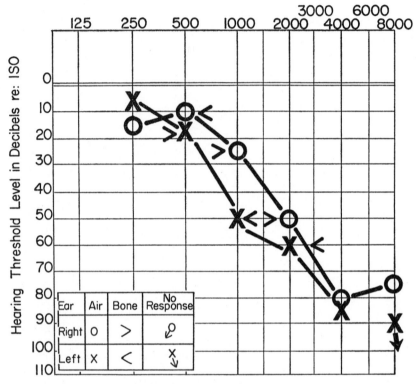

## PURE TONE AUDIOGRAM
### Frequency in Hertz

Figure 5-4. Pure tone audiogram of C. W. showing a mild, bilateral sensorineural hearing loss at one thousand Hz and a more severe loss for the higher frequencies.

rors usually are ones of omission, rather than ones of substitution or distortion.

MILD-TO-MODERATE SENSORINEURAL LOSS: Two different audiometric configurations will be discussed in this section: (a) a flat loss of a moderate degree, and (b) a loss that gradually becomes more severe, from low through the high frequencies.

Speech can be significantly affected by a mild-to-moderate sensorineural hearing loss. Some or all of the errors mentioned previously in this chapter may occur. Vowels are most likely to be correct. Voiceless, high-frequency consonant sounds that are less visible are most likely to be in error. Specific errors vary a great deal with the individual child, but generally, if some acoustic cues are available and used by the child, the phoneme in error will be distorted, or a substitution will be employed. If *no* acoustic or visual cues are available (e.g. the absence of cues for /s/ and /sh/ which may occur with a severe loss above one thousand Hz), the aforementioned phonemes will usually be omitted.

The following cases illustrate the variety of speech errors which frequently occur with mild-to-moderate sensorineural hearing losses:

L. O. was referred for an evaluation at six years of age because of very poor speech. Subsequent audiologic evaluation revealed a sig-

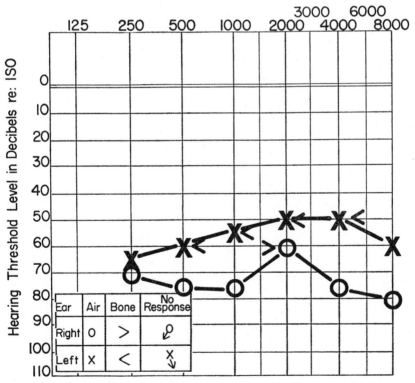

Figure 5-5. Pure tone audiogram of L. O. showing a bilateral, flat sensorineural hearing loss of moderate-to-severe degree.

nificant hearing loss for all frequencies for both ears (Figure 5-5). Analysis of articulation revealed inconsistent omission of medial and final consonant sounds and occasional vowel distortion. Short concrete verbal responses could be understood, but conversation became unintelligible during his attempts to use linguistic patterns which were more complex than he understood.

J. A. had been inappropriately placed in a special education class for mentally retarded children for four years on the basis of delayed language development and unintelligible speech. Audiologic evaluation revealed a significant hearing loss for both ears above two hundred fifty Hz (Figure 5-6). Speech evaluation revealed poor intelligibility of unstructured responses. Error analysis revealed frequent confusion among voiceless stop consonants (/p/, /t/, and /k/) and less visible voiced stops and nasals (/d/, /g/, /n/, and /ng/). Sibilants were distorted.

Amplification may or may not result in direct speech benefits for children in the moderate sensorineural category. When L. O. was fitted with a hearing aid immediate improvement was observed, especially in his ability to correct specific phonemic errors. J. A., who was several years older, appeared only to tolerate amplification, since other children in his class for hearing-impaired children wore hearing aids. Some gradual improvement in speech was observed. This improvement was thought to have resulted from appropriate instruction, rather than from use of the hearing aid.

If the child's hearing is normal or near normal for some portion of the low frequencies, as in the case of J. A., amplified cues from the normal low frequency range may mask or overshadow any amplification for important higher frequency speech cues. Auditory cues may be made available through a hearing aid, but these cues frequently are quite distorted. Therefore, normal hearing in a portion of the frequency range may preclude help for the hearing impaired child by use of a conventional hearing aid. Thus, exploration of the benefit of a special hearing aid (See CROS Aids, Chapter IX) may then be initiated by the audiologist.

In summary, audiologic information for each child, together with acoustic information for all phonetic units, can lead to

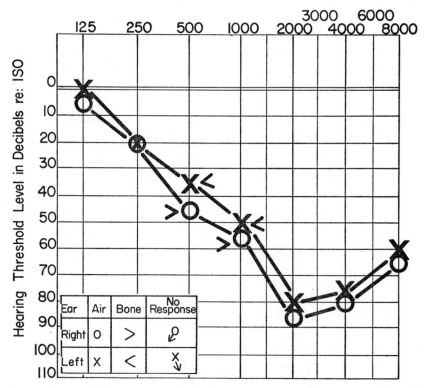

Figure 5-6. Pure tone audiogram of J. A. showing a bilateral sensorineural hearing loss which becomes more severe from low-to-high frequencies.

more accurate analysis of the child's speech errors. This analysis, in turn, leads to more appropriate therapy goals and procedures.

If audiological information is not available, arrangements should be made for an evaluation by an audiologist. Therapy should not be postponed until the audiologist's report is received, but the clinician will need to structure his evaluation of the child's speech to elicit the maximum information in a brief period of time until such audiological information is available.

## SPEECH EVALUATION

As with all children, enrollment of a hearing-impaired child for therapy should only be based on the existence of a speech or language problem that the clinician believes he can help eliminate. Usually this decision cannot be made until a brief but thorough speech and language evaluation is completed by the clinician.

### Obtaining a Speech Sample

If possible, obtain a tape-recorded sample of the child's speech. This will allow a careful analysis of the speech, and none of the child's verbal output will be overlooked. This sample should include speech in several contexts. Rote responses, such as counting, should be obtained. Structured short responses, usually elicited with pictures or familiar objects, should include all parts of speech. Include a stimulus to elicit the telling of a story, and finally, assess the child's ability to carry on a very unstructured conversation.

Additional detailed instructions concerning how to obtain and analyze this type of sample, in terms of language, are given elsewhere in this publication (See Chapter VI).

### Analysis of Speech Errors

Articulation errors, noted in the speech sample described above, can be analyzed by answering a few appropriate questions. The answers to these questions, in turn, will lead to decisions concerning the clinician's emphasis in therapy.

1. *Which phonemes are consistently in error, and do these phonemes have limited auditory and visual features, such as /h/, /s/, /sh/, and /ch/?* Hearing loss limits the use of auditory cues. Errors are more likely to occur on those phonemes that are high in pitch, low in intensity, and short in duration. If the phonemes also lack visual cues, such as /k/ and /h/, they will be difficult for the hearing-impaired child to produce correctly until he learns to use tactile and kinesthetic cues.

2. *What type of error occurs (omission, At for Hat; substitu-*

*tion, Take for Cake; distortion, lateralized /s/)?* Are the substitutions and distortions errors of placement, /t/ for /k/, or voicing, /s/ for /z/? As mentioned previously, low intensity sounds are most frequently omitted, and substitutions occur for stop consonants. As the child becomes aware of each phonetic unit, distortions may increase during his attempts to approximate the correct production. Voiced and voiceless consonants are also frequently confused by the hearing-impaired child because these pairs of phonemes are identical visually.

3. *Is there a pattern for the inconsistent errors?* Do they occur in specific phonetic contexts, such as /t/ for /k/ preceding vowels but never in the final position? Do the errors occur in similar linguistic contexts, for example, /t/ omitted for past tense, as in *stopped?* The latter may be a language error rather than an error in production of the /t/ phoneme. Therapy will differ significantly in each case.

4. *Does the breakdown occur between single words and short phrases, or between structured responses and spontaneous conversation?* The hearing-impaired child frequently has adequate articulation in single syllable words, but errors begin to occur when longer responses are given. As with any child, therapy should emphasize areas of difficulty. Do not stress production of the phoneme in isolation or in single words if the breakdown does not occur until phrases are used.

5. *Are the errors truly speech errors, or do they fall into the grey area where speech and language become inseparable?* The author's experience with hearing-impaired children suggests that errors frequently interpreted as speech errors are directly related to language deficiencies. For example, is the child distorting a final /z/, or does he have difficulty with the concept of singular-plural or pronoun-verb agreement (i.e. I go, you go, he go/z/)?

6. *In analyzing error consistency, does one find a continual record of indistinct speech errors appearing in more complex syntactical responses?* The child with indistinct speech errors may be attempting to use sophisticated linguistic patterns he

has heard, but the specific components of these patterns are not fully understood by him. An attempt to use a connective, a preposition, and an article in the following utterance, is an example of this type of problem: *Me uh Joe play ih-uh football.* When the indistinct speech problem is present, intelligibility decreases significantly in longer and more complex responses. In other words, if the listener cannot understand what the hearing-impaired child has said, there is a high probability that the child is attempting to use an indistinct pattern, rather than misarticulating specific phonetic units. If this is true, the implications for therapy planning are significant, since *language* must be the focus, rather than speech. In addition, one would expect concurrent improvement in speech intelligibility, as increasingly complex linguistic structures are learned by the child.

During the evaluation period, the clinician should make a judgment concerning the *child's* impression of his speech. Is he aware of his errors, and does he attempt to correct them without reminders? Is he reluctant to talk because of poor intelligibility? Does he not respond because he doesn't understand the question or have the appropriate language for a correct response? If the latter is the case, again, deficient language is the primary problem, rather than poor speech.

The child's reactions and ability to benefit from the clinician's stimulation must also be assessed. Which errors are corrected easily in isolation? Can the child incorporate the correct production into single words, short phrases, and sentences? Are there any sounds that the child is unable to produce, no matter what type of stimulation is provided by the clinician?

Finally, in a diagnostic work-up, one must not eliminate consideration of factors other than, or in addition to, hearing loss, i.e. mental retardation, emotional disturbance, perceptual impairment, visual problems, or cleft palate. There is a high incidence of multiple handicaps in the hearing-impaired population, and articulation errors can and do have varied etiologies, even in this population. A different approach during therapy may need to be taken if hearing loss is not the only cause of the speech errors.

A brief oral-motor examination should be completed. Are the child's articulators (lips, tongue, teeth, palate) intact and capable of correct speech production? Is the child functioning at expectancy for his chronological age in nonlanguage areas, or are there other deficiencies which could account for at least a portion of the articulation errors? Does the child relate to others in an appropriate manner for his chronological age, or does his behavior appear immature and/or significantly abnormal?

If an intellectual assessment has been completed, the clinician should be familiar with the results. Intelligence test scores should be interpreted with care. Many psychological tests are so verbally oriented that the hearing-impaired child will not do well and be mislabelled *retarded* (e.g. J. A., Figure 5-6).

In summary, a thorough but necessarily brief evaluation must be completed prior to planning therapy. Diagnosis should be an automatic part of the total therapy program, but answers to the above questions will help clarify a starting point for defining therapy goals and procedures.

## EMPHASIS IN THERAPY

It has been stated repeatedly that many different problems can result from a hearing loss. The clinician may be asked or expected to solve any or all of these problems. As a communication specialist, the clinician must discover the *primary* problem, i.e. the communication deficiency which most directly affects the child's ability to function effectively in all situations.

Speech correction, speechreading, auditory training, and specific academic skills are all important areas to be included, but they should be extensions of a language-oriented therapy program. Thus, one must ask how he can incorporate each of these areas, especially *speech correction,* into a total therapy program to improve the communication ability of the hearing-impaired child.

## SPEECH CORRECTION: GOALS AND GUIDELINES

The primary therapy goal for speech correction is to develop the child's ability to monitor his own output as quickly and effectively as possible. This goal should always be the basis for any specific therapy technique utilized.

If the child's speech is unintelligible to his teacher and his peers, then it becomes a most significant problem that should be dealt with directly. As mentioned earlier, however, a careful analysis of the child's speech pattern frequently reveals poor intelligibility only in specific contexts and with a direct relationship to linguistic or conceptual deficits. In this situation, the child's speech should improve as he begins to understand the linguistic units he is attempting to use, for example, articles, prepositions, and possessives.

If specific phonemes are consistently misarticulated, the child should be shown the correct placement using all cues (visual, auditory, tactile, kinesthetic) available. Following this, the child should be encouraged to modify his production of the sound, with as little direct stimulation by the clinician as possible. Close approximations of the correct production should be reinforced when they are improvements over previous attempts.

Ear training is frequently the first step in traditional programs for correcting articulation errors. If the child's hearing loss is such that he cannot identify and discriminate specific phonemes by auditory cues alone, traditional ear training activities will be frustrating and nonproductive. Techniques described in Chapter VIII on auditory training will usually be more beneficial for the hearing-impaired child.

As stated previously, *therapy should be language-based, with speech improvement as an extension.* Drill on phoneme production in nonsense syllables is usually inappropriate and unnecessary for the hearing-impaired child. Production in single syllable words is much preferred, since it can also be related to needed vocabulary development. Language activities can be designed to include vocabulary containing a specific sound that needs practice. For example, the voiced /th/ sound would be used frequently when working on plural pronouns such as *they, them, these* and *those.*

The clinician should be aware of the principles of reinforcement (Blackwood, 1971), and these principles should be a carefully designed part of the therapy program. Immediate reinforcement with appropriate rewards is necessary for achieving positive transfer and carry over outside the therapy situation.

With limited therapy time available, the clinician cannot afford to ignore any correct production of the target phoneme, but care should be taken that the child does not become focused on the reward, rather than the therapy objective.

The guidelines proposed for articulation errors also apply to problems with voice and rhythm. If the child's habitual pitch is inappropriate, he should be given visual and kinesthetic cues to assist him in modifying his pitch. Phrasing and inflection patterns are directly related to the meaning of the utterance. Thus, therapy for problems in these areas cannot be separated from language-oriented activities.

Finally, the clinician must be flexible in utilizing therapy techniques. Behavioral objectives (Mager, 1962) are extremely useful for measuring progress. If the child continually fails to achieve the criteria for success, either the objective is unrealistic, or the technique being used is inappropriate. In either case, a modification is needed. It should be made whenever this continued failure is recognized. While all hearing-impaired children have the factor of hearing loss in common, each child is an individual. Each may require a different approach to achieve identical goals.

## THERAPY OUTSIDE THE THERAPY SETTING

The language used during therapy should always be correlated with that being used in the child's classroom. It must be relevant to his daily environment. Therefore, classroom observation can be very revealing and beneficial for the clinician. If time is not available for this purpose, perhaps one scheduled therapy session each month should be replaced by classroom observation and teacher consultation.

### *Classroom Observation*

Observation should include the child's interaction with his teacher and his peers, general classroom behavior, and his performance and participation in class activities relative to the following: (a) can he follow directions given to the entire class? (b) does his understanding improve when the teacher repeats instructions individually? (c) does the child complete tasks independently? (d) can he follow class discussions? (e) are there any activities where he is not required to participate? (f) is his intelligibility so poor that teachers and peers cannot understand his oral responses? and (g) does the material being taught include a great deal of vocabulary that he does not comprehend?

The child's performance in a structured therapy session is often quite different from his performance elsewhere. Answers to the previously cited questions will help the clinician determine specific needs for therapy and evaluate carry-over of progress which has been observed within the therapy setting.

### *Teacher and Parent Consultation*

Confusion and lack of knowledge of the therapy process, reported by Eisenstadt (1972), are frequently found within the public school, as well as in the home. Eisenstadt's informal investigation revealed that parents were frequently uncertain about the reasons for therapy, the progress being made, and what supportive assistance should be given at home. Teachers, too, often are poorly informed and unaware of even the broader speech therapy goals.

The clinician should involve the classroom teacher as much as possible and provide him with current information concerning therapy objectives. It is most important that the teacher know the target phoneme, vocabulary, or language concept so that additional reinforcement for correct usage can be provided in the classroom. However, demands on the teacher must be realistic. Classroom structure does not allow time for extensive individual instruction for any child. However, if the clinician has coordinated the therapy objectives with the current academic goals, there will be many opportunities for the teacher to reinforce success and thus increase the child's rate of progress.

Parents should also be involved as much as possible and be informed of both general and specific therapy goals for their child, for they can also provide reinforcement at home.

### SUMMARY

Information from acoustical research can provide the clinician with certain expectations concerning the speech of a child with a hearing loss. However, each hearing-impaired child is an individual and should be evaluated as such. Acoustical information cannot be meaningful unless an audiogram is available to provide an idea of which frequencies are or are not being heard during normal conversation. If amplification is being used, there is a high probability that the child is still receiving acoustic distortion which can affect his speech production.

The clinician must be aware of all possible problem areas for each hearing-impaired child. Additional handicapping conditions frequently magnify speech and language problems related to the existing hearing loss and may change the clinician's decision concerning approaches to therapy.

A careful analysis of the child's speech and language should precede decisions concerning therapy objectives. *Articulation frequently is not the most significant deficiency for the hearing-impaired child, and, therefore, often deserves less emphasis than other problem areas. In general, therapy should be language-based, with speech improvement incorporated into the broader therapy goals.*

Therapy materials should be relevant to the child's environment, and techniques should be appropriate and reinforcing. The clinician should outline a program with specific therapy objectives and then be flexible enough to modify this program if it becomes inappropriate.

Communication between the clinician and classroom teacher should be an ongoing integral part of the therapy process. The classroom teacher, as well as the child's parents, can be invaluable. They should be provided with appropriate information concerning the child's present limitations and realistic expectations of his performance in the regular classroom.

When the clinician's time is limited, he must make maximum use of all resources available in the hearing-impaired child's environment. This fact cannot be overemphasized. It should never be forgotten that the major speech therapy goal is to develop the child's ability to monitor his own output. This must be done as quickly as possible so that the clinician can become a guide for the child in the design of therapy techniques for his use outside of the limited therapy sessions.

## REFERENCES

Anderson, V. A.: *Improving the Child's Speech.* New York, Oxford, 1953.

Annual Survey of Hearing Impaired Children and Youth. *Additional Handicapping Conditions, Age at Onset of Hearing Loss, and Other Characteristics of Hearing Impaired Students.* Series D, No. 3. Washington, D. C., Gallaudet College, June 1970.

Berg, F. S., and Fletcher, S. G. (Eds.): *The Hard of Hearing Child.* New York, Grune and Stratton, 1970.

Blackwood, Ralph O.: *Operant Control of Behavior.* Akron, Exordium Press, 1971.

Davis, H., and Silverman, S. R. (Eds.): *Hearing and Deafness.* New York, Holt, Rinehart and Winston, 1960.

Eisenstadt, A. A.: Weakness in clinical procedures—a parental evaluation. *ASHA, 14:*1, 1972.

Gardner, H. J.: Application of a high-frequency consonant discrimination word list in hearing-aid evaluation. *J Speech Hearing Dis, 36:*354, 1971.

Lawrence, D. L., and Byers, V. W.: Identification of voiceless fricatives by high-frequency hearing impaired listeners. *J Speech Hearing Res, 12:* 426, 1969.

Locke, J. L.: Discriminative learning in children's acquisition of phonology. *J. Speech Hearing Res, 11:*428, 1968.

McDonald, E. T.: *Articulation Testing and Treatment: A Sensory-Motor Approach.* Pittsburgh, Stanwix House, 1964.

Mager, R. F.: *Preparing Instructional Objectives.* Palo Alto, Fearon Publishers, 1962.

Mowrer, D. E.: Evaluation speech therapy through precision recording. *J Speech Hearing Dis, 34:*239, 1969.

Mowrer, D. E.: Transfer of training in articulation therapy. *J Speech Hearing Dis, 36:*427, 1971.

Newby, H. A.: *Audiology.* New York, Appleton-Century-Crofts, 1964.

Oliver, R., Zelko, H., and Holtzman, P.: *Communicative Speaking and Listening.* New York, Holt, Rinehart and Winston, 1968.

Prins, D.: Relations among articulatory deviations and responses to a clinical measure of sound discrimination ability. *J Speech Hearing Dis, 28:* 382, 1963.

Sanders, D. A.: *Aural Rehabilitation.* New Jersey, Prentice-Hall, 1970.

Sanders, D. A., and Goodrich, S. J.: The relative contribution of visual and auditory components of speech intelligibility as a function of three conditions of frequency distortion. *J Speech Hearing Res, 14:*154, 1971.

# CHAPTER VI

# LANGUAGE EVALUATION OF HEARING-IMPAIRED STUDENTS: A PRAGMATIC APPROACH

## Verna Yater and Jackie Simms

O RDERLY PROGRESSION and variation in language acquisition is characteristic of the hard-of-hearing student just as it is for the normal-hearing student. However, some problems of language acquisition are more unique to the hearing-impaired student because of the impact of hearing loss on his auditory input.

The hearing-impaired student typically can be expected to have problems in the areas of oral and written language. Generally, he may be expected to lag several years behind his normal hearing peers in language and related skills. This is particularly true if detection of the hearing loss was delayed and if intervention in the form of amplification and intensive education was not begun early.

It is the purpose of this chapter to outline some problem areas of language development encountered by the hearing-impaired student and to suggest methods to evaluate these areas. Only evaluation techniques which can be done in an educational setting will be considered. These techniques are designed to identify problem areas and to establish base lines of performance for use in evaluating the effectiveness of therapy.

## OVERVIEW OF THE LANGUAGE PROBLEMS OF THE HEARING-IMPAIRED CHILD

While the hearing-impaired child may experience many types of language problems, some problems appear to be more typical than others. The most common types of language problems experienced by the school-aged, hearing-impaired child are (a) speech errors, (b) oral language difficulties, (c) written language difficulties, (d) vocabulary deficiencies, (e) difficulties with organizational skills, and (f) difficulties in comprehension of written directions. All of these problem areas are interrelated and affect each other. However, they will be considered separately for ease of discussion.

Common speech errors of the hearing-impaired child are omissions and substitutions particularly of high frequency sounds. These articulation problems represent speech errors, but they also have a great impact on the child's language skills.

The hearing-impaired student's oral language skills will frequently reflect his speech problems as well as his difficulty in accurate reception of vocabulary concepts and correct use of syntactical structures. Words which are phonetically difficult to perceive are often omitted. Function words, i.e. words whose main role is to assist in the structure of a sentence, are frequently omitted.

Production of written language by the hearing-impaired student will be similar to his oral language. In some cases, the severity of the problem may even be greater in this area. Vocabulary deficiency, as well as poor morphological and syntactical structures which occur in his oral language, will also be present in his written language. Also, he may not understand basic sentence format or may misunderstand transformation or the internal structural components of sentences. In some instances, the student may have partially correct oral language but not yet be capable of written language production.

Vocabulary concepts will often be erroneously perceived and therefore, misused by the hearing-impaired student. Vocabulary referents which have been misperceived will limit comprehension of written material, and extended or multiple meanings of words are often absent in his verbal and written production.

Miscellaneous skills such as organizational skills and the ability to understand written directions will also often be affected by a hearing loss. Poor functioning in these areas will inhibit the student's performance on certain subsections of standardized achievement tests. These miscellaneous skills are pertinent to the student's functioning in an academic environment. Because of their relevance and influence on many academic tasks, they must be evaluated when considering the language problems of the hearing-impaired student.

The extent and severity of the hearing-impaired student's language problem is related to the degree of his hearing loss, his intellectual capability, his academic training and intrinsic motivation. Other factors may play a role in a particular student's language development. For example, speech, a prior and concomitant skill, is one such factor which is important to the development and improvement of the hearing-impaired student's language skills.

## EFFECTS OF SPEECH ERRORS
## ON LANGUAGE DEVELOPMENT AND USAGE

In this chapter, speech will be considered as the conveyor of language. While the importance of articulation is recognized, neither the assessment nor correction of articulation *per se* will be considered.

If a child's speech production is poor, his language concepts and production cannot be expected to be much better. While certain language concepts will develop beyond the child's speech capabilities, faulty speech will hinder language development. Uncorrected speech errors will adversely affect his language competency.

The hearing-impaired student's speech patterns will reflect his inability to hear in certain frequency ranges. For example, it is not unusual for the student with a moderate, bilateral, high frequency loss to be unaware that a sibilant has been uttered. If the student with such a hearing impairment is unaware of the /s/, /es/, /z/, and /ez/, phonemes, he may perceive and say, for example, *Dyonym are word that mean the same thing* instead of *Synonyms are words that mean the same thing.*

Errors of oral and written language related to noun-plural affixes, past-tense suffixes and subject-verb agreement can be attributed, in part, to his limited ability to hear and reproduce speech correctly. Also, vocabulary acquisition and reading skill can be negatively influenced by his speech errors. Speech errors influence the hearing-impaired student's development in diverse ways. Therefore, these errors should be corrected as readily as possible to improve his language growth.

### Effects of Speech Errors on Noun-Plural Affixes and Past Tense Suffixes

Speech misarticulation and omissions, particularly of the endings /s/, /es/, /z/, /ez/, /t/, /d/, and /ed/, affect the hearing-impaired student's language performance. Misused noun-plural affixes and past tense suffixes which might be classified as typical language errors may be attributable to the child's problems with misperceived speech. For example, the child might say:

1. *She wash her hands with soap powder.* The final /t/ was omitted from the word *washed*.
2. *Mother think we'll visit California this summer.* The final /s/ was omitted from the word *thinks*.
3. *I jump on the trampoline yesterday.* The final /t/ was omitted from the word *jumped*.
4. *Mary love the toy dish and tiny paper napkin.* The final /d/ from the word *loved*, the final /ez/ from *dishes* and the final /z/ from *napkins* were omitted.

Helping the child develop good discrimination skills and directing his visual attention to affixes and suffixes will improve both speech and language skills.

### Influences of Speech Errors on Plural Usage and Subject-Verb Agreement

The /s/, /es/, /z/, and /ez/ phonemes are of great importance in the English language. Their omission affects not only plural usage but also subject-verb agreement. A student who does not hear and, therefore, does not use these sounds, may show a multitude of language errors.

Some examples of common plural misusage and subject-verb agreement errors often made by the hearing-impaired student are as follows:

1. *Mother drink coffee.* This is a classic example of the omission

of the final /s/ phoneme on a verb which makes the sentence grammatically incorrect.

2. *Some ball.* In this case, the child omitted the final /z/ phoneme. The error is a lack of pluralization of the word *ball.*
3. *Antonyms are word that means opposite thing.* Inconsistent usage of pluralization and incorrect subject-verb agreement are common in children who are in the process of learning to incorporate these rules into their verbal language. It is not unusual for a hard-of-hearing child who has had some work in singular and plural nouns and subject-verb agreement to make this type of error.
4. *Our mother was here.* For the child who cannot hear the final /z/, the leap from *our mother was* to *our mothers were* is monumental. The child who doesn't perceive the /z/ which is, in this case, the transmitter of the meaning, i.e. more than one mother, does not automatically realize that he will have to change the verb form.

Systematic teaching of subject-verb agreement and rules of usage of plurals will help the hearing-impaired student to use these language forms correctly.

### *Effect of Speech Errors on Vocabulary*

Vocabulary is often learned through context directly from a speaker. A person with normal hearing is exposed to various words many times in numerous ways. Although he may, at first, be unsure of their meanings, he can generally articulate the words and gradually perceive their meanings.

A hearing loss will make it difficult to accurately perceive the spoken word, thus, making new vocabulary acquisition difficult. Because the student misperceives and misarticulates speech, he will have further problems. He will incorrectly produce new words that he considers correct. The child who misarticulates certain phonemes because of his hearing loss, may have difficulty acquiring new vocabulary words which incorporate his misarticulated phonemes.

Not only is it often difficult for the student with a hearing loss to perceive new vocabulary words auditorially, it may also be difficult for him to learn new words through speechreading. It is often difficult to speechread a new word the first time it is seen because some phonemes look exactly alike. For example, /d/, /t/, /n/, and /l/ look almost identical. Unless he can lipread accompanying contextual clues, the child who sees *low* might perceive it as *tow, know, no, doe,* or *dough.* If he is unfamiliar with the meaning of some of the words, his task will be further complicated. A big variation of meaning would be conveyed by: They found Brad's toe (*They found Brad's doe* or *They found Brad's dough*).

### *Influence of Speech Errors on Reading*

Articulation problems related to a hearing loss may also affect the development of the child's reading skills. The child who does not perceive or articulate some phonemes in his verbal communication may find learning to read, especially sound-symbol association skills, a herculean task. Intervention in the form of amplification and individualized instruction will help to circumvent difficulties with the acquisition of good phonic skills.

The hearing-impaired child who has difficulty producing a single or multisyllabic word in conversation will have similar problems in oral reading. During the primary years, much reading practice is done orally. The child learns some reading skills through the teacher's reinforcement of his verbal responses. If his speech is poor, it may be difficult to understand what he is saying. If a teacher is uncertain of what has been said, she may be reluctant or unable to correct the child's oral reading; therefore, his errors may be perpetuated.

A hearing-impaired student's reading comprehension may be poor because he has a limited vocabulary. Also, he may have learned faulty meanings for word symbols and will attach erroneous meaning to what he has read. He may not adequately recognize certain syntactical structures because he is unfamiliar with them. He may, therefore, not fully comprehend some written materials.

The role of speech in language development cannot be overlooked nor its importance underestimated. The child with a hearing loss will need help to overcome speech deficiencies. If speech errors are left uncorrected, they will not automatically disappear. Indeed, language areas will be greatly affected by their presence.

## ORAL LANGUAGE MEASUREMENT

The hard-of-hearing child usually has more difficulty developing oral language skills than the child with normal hearing because of misperceptions, lack of vocabulary development, limited understanding and poor usage of syntactical structures. Therefore, an evaluation of oral language should explore these potential problem areas.

### *Obtaining an Oral Language Sample*

In the interest of convenience and simplicity, it is suggested that an oral language sample be obtained by having the student tell a story using a picture stimulus. The picture should contain considerable action to insure elicitation of an adequate language sample. Figure 6-1 shows an action picture which would be appropriate for use in obtaining an oral language sample.

The student's story should be tape recorded. This will enable the clinician to carefully analyze the language sample.

The verbal instructions given to the student should be as follows: *I am going to show you a picture. I want you to tell the best story you can about the picture.* The picture should be shown to the child for a few seconds, the instructions repeated, and then the tape recorder turned on.

The student should be prompted as little as possible after the instructions are understood. An occasional *what* or *why* encouragement might be used if the child stops talking before an adequate sample is obtained.

To insure accuracy in transcribing the child's taped response, it may, at times, be helpful for the clinician to take notes on the child's story, particularly if he has many speech errors. Transcription of the recorded story should be done as soon as possible after collection of the story.

An oral language sample of at least fifty utterances (Johnson,

Figure 6-1. Example of an action picture which could be used to obtain an oral language sample.

Darley and Spriesterbach, 1963) should yield a sample which will provide a functional language profile.

### Analysis of the Oral Language Sample

Transcription of the student's oral language responses into written form is the first step in its analysis. A modification of the method of analyzing oral language, as suggested by Johnson, Darley and Spriesterbach (1963), is appropriate.

SENTENCE ANALYSIS: Analysis of the sample can be done by classifying the student's oral output into basic categories. From these categories sentence strengths and weaknesses can be determined. The *seven response categories* given below are based on a simple to more complex language progression. Classification of the student's sentences by using these categories will provide a relative guideline of the complexity of his sentence responses.

The following seven types of response categories will provide a broad indication of the student's sentence development:

1. *Naming only.* The use of a noun or other single word with no modifiers of any type, i.e. trunk, baseball, chair.
2. *Listing.* The use of words with modifiers, i.e. a dog, the model, some boys, five balloons.
3. *Functionally and structurally incomplete responses,* i.e. A girl got a fish and her cat she did and it scared at. Gonna do, oh, get it at.
4. *Functionally complete, but structurally incomplete or incorrect responses,* i.e. He wearing old clothes. Bobby play checkers.
5. *Simple sentences without phrases,* i.e. They wept; Tommy left.
6. *Simple sentences with phrases,* i.e. He has about ten balloons in his hand; Mom and Dad are eating dinner; Dad brought Bob and Mary some balloons.
7. *Compound or complex sentences,* i.e. The girl played with her balloon and the dog barked at her; Mr. and Mrs. Smith, parents of Linda, a ninth grade student, attended the meeting.

By classifying the hard-of-hearing student's oral output, as indicated above, and by tabulating use and percentages for each category, a quick view of any weakness of word, phrase, and sentence structure is apparent and quantified.

Sufficient basic information for long-range therapy planning and measurement can usually be attained by repeating the oral language sample at six to twelve month intervals.

Below is a transcribed oral language sample obtained from a ten year old, hard-of-hearing, fourth grade girl. Following each sentence, in parenthesis, is a number from one to seven indicating the unit or sentence complexity, i.e. response category as was described above. Table 6-I shows a summary of the analysis of this sample.

One day a family went on a picnic (6). And a man pumps up some balloons for the children (6). A, man got a frog and his dog he did

............ and it scared at (3). And the children are playing with their balloon, too (4). The boy has a boat on his balloon and the girl has a doll on hers (7). And here come the balloon man (4). He was so happy (5). And then the, then the dog, the dog start looking at the balloon that, that that the family have (4). The dog had jumped on them and trying to pop it (4). And then the children ranned over where, by another playground (4). There's a whole bunch of trees by the man (6). And there is food on the picnic table (4). And the childrens are wearing good clothes (4). Except the boy isn't (4). He wearing old clothes (4). The boy, the man is wear, wearing some good clothes, too, I guess (4). And the dog starts run around (4). The grass is green (5). And the man got a hat on with the balloon (4). He has 'bout ten balloons in his hand (6).

A glimpse at Table 6-I shows that this student has a preponderance of functionally complete, but structurally incomplete or incorrect responses. In other words, the meaning is clear to the listener, but the syntactical structure is incomplete or incorrect. The fact that there were no *naming only* or *listing* responses is a good indication that oral language output is essentially beyond the naming or listing level.

One might suspect that the great number of type four responses, *functionally complete but structurally incomplete sentences,* may be due to the student's exploration and attempts to

TABLE 6-I

PRAGMATIC SENTENCE ANALYSIS OF A FOURTH GRADE
HEARING-IMPAIRED STUDENT'S ORAL LANGUAGE

|  | *Sentence Response Categories* | *Number of Responses* | *Percent of Total Responses* |
|---|---|---|---|
| 1. | Naming only | 0 | 0 |
| 2. | Listing | 0 | 0 |
| 3. | Functionally and structurally incomplete or incorrect responses | 1 | 5 |
| 4. | Functionally complete, but structurally incomplete or incorrect responses | 12 | 60 |
| 5. | Simple sentences without phrases | 2 | 10 |
| 6. | Simple sentences with phrases | 4 | 20 |
| 7. | Compound or complex sentences | 1 | 5 |
|  | Total | 20 | 100 |

TABLE 6-II

FORMAT FOR RECORDING INTERNAL SENTENCE ERRORS

| Internal Errors | Correct Use | Number of Times |
|---|---|---|
| Verbs: | | |
| Present tense | . . . . . . . . . . . . . . . . . . | . . . . . . . . . . . . . . . . . . |
| Past tense | . . . . . . . . . . . . . . . . . . | . . . . . . . . . . . . . . . . . . |
| Future time | . . . . . . . . . . . . . . . . . . | . . . . . . . . . . . . . . . . . . |
| Describe verb usage errors | . . . . . . . . . . . . . . . . . . | . . . . . . . . . . . . . . . . . . |
| Pronouns: | . . . . . . . . . . . . . . . | . . . . . . . . . . . . . . . . . . |
| Describe errors . . . . . . . . . . . . . | | |
| Wh Question Forms | | |
| What . . . . . . . . . . . . . . . . . . . . . . | | |
| Who . . . . . . . . . . . . . . . . . . . . . . | | |
| Where . . . . . . . . . . . . . . . . . . . . | | |
| When . . . . . . . . . . . . . . . . . . . . | | |
| Why . . . . . . . . . . . . . . . . . . . . . | | |
| How . . . . . . . . . . . . . . . . . . . . . | | |

use simple sentences with and without phrases. Looking at the transcribed oral language sample, it is apparent that therapy efforts should be geared toward providing opportunities for practice in producing structurally complete and correct sentences.

INTERNAL STRUCTURAL ANALYSIS: By analyzing the problem areas within the sentence structure, both the student and clinician have definitive knowledge of what aspects of oral language need strengthening. Thus, internal structural analysis, or analysis of the parts of a sentence, is the second step in oral language assessment.

All types of internal structures of the student's oral language sample can be analyzed, but (a) verb and verb-tense usage, (b) correct and incorrect use of pronouns, and (c) use of question forms are those errors which are most commonly encountered in a hearing-impaired student's oral language.

A format is given in Table 6-II for recording the aforementioned sentence structure errors. The format provides spaces for recording verb usage, pronoun usage, and *wh* question form usage.

*Verb and Verb Tense Usage.* Verb usage, particularly the correct use of some past tenses, is a common problem of students with a hearing impairment. A hearing loss diminishes the ability to hear /d/, /ed/, or /t/, i.e. endings of many verbs in past tense forms. Therefore, the past tense of a verb is often heard as present tense. For example, the student hears *enjoy* instead of *enjoyed, visit* instead of *visited,* or *adore* instead of *adored.*

The hearing-impaired student may not be aware that there are many verbs that add /ed/ to form the past tense since he does not hear the forms. He may be unaware that the pronunciation of /ed/ is dependent on the sound preceding the suffix. He may not know that /ed/ is pronounced as /t/ after /p/, /k/, /f/, /s/, /sh/, and /ch/, as for example in past tense of *hop, talk, laugh, hiss, wash, watch.* He may not know that /ed/ is pronounced as /d/ after voiced consonants and vowels. For example, past tense of *mob, lag, love, raze, judge, yell,* or *lie* are pronounced as /d/. And he may be unaware that /ed/ is pronounced as /ed/ after /t/ or /d/ as for example in *protect* or *land.*

In addition to often not hearing past tense verb forms, the hearing-impaired student may not associate time phrases such as yesterday, last week, or this morning with verb usage or with patterning for the past tense.

The hearing-impaired student may, of course, have verb usage difficulties other than with those of the past tense. Errors should be analyzed to see whether there are clusters of errors. If such clusters exist, the clinician can then provide the student with practice in correct usage.

The clinician may want to reclarify his own understanding of English grammar by review of practical guides such as those by Cattell (1972) or Streng (1972).

*Pronoun Usage.* Incorrect pronoun usage is another common oral language difficulty of the hearing-impaired student. His diminished ability to hear the portion of words which are pluralized by the /s/, /es/, /z/, and /ez/ phonemes can contribute to this problem.

If one cannot hear or does not use the /z/ at the end of the word *boys,* he is less likely to learn that sometimes the pronoun for *boy* (as he hears it) is *he* and other times it is *they.* Difficulties caused by this confusion are similar when possessive pronouns are used. For example, *the boy's bats* could easily be confused by the child who might not hear the plural /s/ on bats. Thus, he may use the singular instead of the plural form. In the example, *The boy(s) went fishing, He caught a lot of fish, His pole broke,* if a child did not perceive the final /z/ on *boys,* in *The boys went fishing,* he would then more or less logically use *he caught* instead of *they caught.* He would also more or less logically use *his pole* instead of *their poles.*

*Question Forms.* Question form errors, i.e. the inability to ask a question in a grammatically correct way, is another common language problem for the hearing-impaired student. This aspect of language may be more slowly learned by the child who has a hearing loss even though he may have been frequently exposed to questions and be able to answer them.

Question forms, as one type of grammatical transformation, may be relatively difficult for all children to handle successfully in early stages of language development. The child with a hearing loss may find this structure even more difficult because of confusion of his incomplete incoming auditory messages and because others in his environment may give him less verbal practice or fewer chances to ask questions.

He may, for example, be able to answer the questions *When did you go?* or *What time is it?* but be unable to formulate the same type of questions himself. Of course, the hearing-impaired child whose language development is still at a low level of development may not adequately comprehend these questions.

One method of assessing a child's question form capabilities is to have the child ask simple questions about an object or representation. The level of difficulty of the question will depend on the particular question form being tested (i.e. *what, where, who, when, why, how*), the age, grade and other language capabilities of the student. For example, testing the use of the question *what* may be done by having the child guess what kind of surprise object a clinician is holding.

The child is told he must ask questions to try to guess what the surprise object is. For example, a clinician might be holding a balloon. The child is instructed to first ask questions that are general and go on to specific questions. The child might say: *What is it made of? Is it big or little? What do you do with it?* The form which the child is learning is kept on a card or sheet of paper so he can see it.

In testing the *who* form, the clinician might use real pictures or stick figures. The child is instructed to ask *who* questions about the people on the pictures. All of the pictures used should be meaningful to the child.

The child's knowledge of the *where* form can be tested by using real or facsimile pictures of places. His concept of *when* can be tested by use of small clock dials which the student can manipulate. *Why* and *how* usage can be assessed from pictures drawn by a clinician to suit the child's age and capability level.

If a child habitually omits any of the *who, what, where, when,* and *how* questions, he should be prompted by the clinician to ask the type of question form usage he has omitted. If he consistently appears not to use a particular question form or be unable to use it, more testing, as suggested above, should be done.

Notation should be made of whether simple question forms are present and correct as well as when more complex question forms are being used by the child. For example, note that the child says, *Who is the people who gave to your mother?* incorrectly, but uses *Who gave it to you?* a simpler *who* question correctly.

Approaches to question form testing as outlined by Carol Chomsky (1969) may be helpful to the clinician. It includes a section about ask/tell which the clinician might modify to her own particular needs.

Question form usage in relation to the child's total language functioning must be left to the clinician's interpretative and creative ability. Standardization of a means of assessment and norms for the development of usage of question form are needed. However, hearing-impaired children in middle elementary grades should be able to use question forms correctly if they are functioning in regular schools.

## WRITTEN LANGUAGE MEASUREMENT

Written language is acquired by the normal hearing child after he has already developed a verbal language system. There is reciprocity between the child's oral and written language output. If his oral language is poorly developed, this will be reflected or magnified in his written language skills.

Many hearing-impaired children have problems with correct verb usage in written language. They are also prone to incorrect usage of the past tense because of the inability to hear the production of or differentiate between either /d/ or /t/.

Omissions of word endings are not unusual for the child with a hearing loss. Word endings are easily misperceived or heard distortedly. Words of one syllable may not be readily perceived; therefore, they are often omitted in writing. Also, contractions are not perceived from oral interaction and are therefore often deleted or misused.

A typical extended language error of hard-of-hearing children is that of a lack of proper punctuation resulting in run-on sentences. Directly related to run-on sentences are capitalization errors. The hearing-impaired student may also make other habitual errors regardless of whether they are identifiable as errors common to hearing-impaired children.

### Obtaining a Written Sample

It is important to evaluate the hard-of-hearing student's written language in terms of total output (number of words and sentences), type of output (complexity), sentence structure, and internal structure for adequate pinpointing of the student's therapy needs. Therefore, these areas of written language should be analyzed in terms of phrase and sentence structure, internal structural errors and developmental syntax from written language samples.

A story written by the student while viewing a stimulus picture can be used for written language sampling purposes. The method of obtaining the sample is similar to that described in the previous section on obtaining an oral language sample.

### Written Language Analysis

The amount and kind of student's written output will be some indicator of his functional language capability. The number of words which a student produces is grossly indicative of the development of his written language (Johnson, Darley and Spriesterbach, 1963). However, the number of sentences a student produces may not increase as much as the number of words produced. Thus, as a student's written language increases in complexity, words-per-sentence will generally increase. Complexity is usually added by phrases and descriptive or delineating words.

An analysis of the student's written language should include a sentence analysis similar to that previously shown in Table 6-I. The response categories used for the written sentence analysis will be identical to those discussed in the previous section (Table 6-I) dealing with oral language output.

A sample of a hearing-impaired student's written language production is given below. The story was in response to a picture shown to the student.

> One day a girl was playing with her doll and her doll house (6). The doll is going to eat her cupcake (4). The girl colored some pictures (5). She has a dog name peewee (4). She play with her dog a lot of time (4). Her father and mother peek in her room (4). Her mother watch her play (4). The girl's hair is yellow and her eyes are blue (7). The girl's name is Patty (4). She have a lot of fun (4).

Note that at the end of each sentence is a number. This number corresponds to one of the seven response categories previously described in the analysis of oral language samples (Table 6-I) and represents the same error categories for written language.

Table 6-III summarizes an analysis of the student's story. Note that most responses from this sample fell into the fourth response category, i.e. functionally complete but structurally incomplete or incorrect responses. The student also attempted to produce simple sentences with phrases but did so either incor-

TABLE 6-III

A PRAGMATIC SENTENCE ANALYSIS OF THE WRITTEN STORY
OF A HEARING-IMPAIRED STUDENT*

| Sentence Response Categories | Number of Responses | Percent of Total Responses |
|---|---|---|
| 1. Naming only | 0 | 0 |
| 2. Listing | 0 | 0 |
| 3. Functionally and structurally incomplete or incorrect responses | 0 | 0 |
| 4. Functionally complete, but structurally incomplete or incorrect responses | 7 | 70 |
| 5. Simple sentences without phrases | 1 | 10 |
| 6. Simple sentences with phrases | 1 | 10 |
| 7. Compound or complex sentences | 1 | 10 |
| Totals | 10 | 100 |

*Note that the majority of errors occur in the fourth response category.

rectly or incompletely. Also verb tense agreement errors resulted in classification of several responses as incorrect.

The above described analysis used periodically will afford the clinician an opportunity to monitor the student's long range progress in written language production. For the measurement of short term progress, a monthly or more frequent analysis such as is described in the following section will suffice.

LANGUAGE ERROR ANALYSIS CHART: Longitudinal progress in written language development can be simply and effectively plotted on a Language Error Analysis Chart as is shown in Table 6-IV.

A profile of progress plotted on the Error Analysis chart, including initial and all subsequent analyses, is helpful to efficiently note the areas in which the student is experiencing language problems as well as the areas in which he is making progress.

The Language Error Analysis Chart (Table 6-IV) contains categories for recording of information regarding written production of words and sentences, usage of verbs and pronouns, and use of punctuation and capitalization.

TABLE 6-IV

WRITTEN LANGUAGE ERROR ANALYSIS CHART

| Date of Evaluation | Sentences | Words | | | Plural Errors | Verbs* | | | Pronoun | | Punctuation | | | | Capitalization | | Totals Exclusive of Sentences | Notation of Other Errors |
|---|---|---|---|---|---|---|---|---|---|---|---|---|---|---|---|---|---|---|
| | Incomplete or Incorrect | Additions | Omissions | Substitutions | | Form | Tense | Agreement | Usage | Antecedent | Period or Question Mark | Comma | Apostrophe | Other | Sentence | Proper Nouns | | |
| October 19 | 0 | 1 | 0 | 0 | 0 | 0 | 4 | 4 | 0 | 0 | 0 | 0 | 0 | | 0 | 1 | | Deleted Hyphen |

* First entry shows that the student's primary difficulty is with verb tense and agreement usage.

The following section provides a brief description and examples of the error categories given in Table 6-IV.

1. Sentence production errors are simply recorded in terms of *incompleteness* or *incorrectness,* e.g. Going to school on Monday (or) They play on a soccer last Tuesday.
2. Errors in word production can include:
   *Additions, e.g.* My lion he growled;
   *Omissions,* e.g. He went the movie;
   *Substitutions,* e.g. Alicia went over their;
   *Plural errors,* e.g. The two hat blew away.
3. Verb usage errors include the following:
   *Form,* e.g. Bring for brought or ranned for ran;
   *Agreement,* e.g. They was hungry;
   *Tense,* i.e. inappropriate tense shift within or between sentences.
4. Pronoun error categories include the following:
   *Usage,* e.g. It was her (or) He did it hisself;
   *Ambiguous Antecedent,* e.g. John and Jack were there and he saw him do it (or) They were in school and he saw it happen.
5. Punctuation errors include the following:
   *Period,* i.e. omission of period after the sentence or abbreviation inappropriately punctuated.
   *Comma,* e.g. Carol likes to swim sculpt, paint and read.
   *Apostrophe misusage* and *other punctuation errors.*
6. Capitalization errors include the following:
   *Beginning of sentences without capitalization and no capitalization of proper nouns.*

Observable writing errors which may not fit into a category should be recorded in either the margin of the chart or indicated on the bottom of the student's language sample. The actual writing sample from which judgments are made should be saved and attached to the chart each time it is used.

The following language sample has been analyzed and recorded in Table 6-IV:

One day a girl was playing with her doll and her house. The doll is going to eat her cupcake. The girl colored some pictures. She has a dog name peewee. She play with her dog a lot of time. Her father and mother peek in her room. Her mother watch her play. The girl's hair is yellow and her eyes are blue. The girl name is Patty. She have a lot of fun.

Note that the student produced ten complete sentences. Word usage showed one addition and no substitutions or omissions. Four errors were noted in verb tense usage and four in verb agreement. There were no punctuation errors. One capitalization error was noted.

An examination of the student's production and the error analysis chart (Table 6-IV) clearly indicates that this student needs remediation in the area of verb usage.

The Error Analysis Chart should be used at specific periodic intervals such as once a month, every six weeks, or every several months. Language samples of the same length (of at least fifty words) should be analyzed at the same predetermined time intervals so that longitudinal changes or growth in written language can be seen at a glance.

All of the language measurement techniques described so far have been nonstandardized. In the following section a brief description of a test standardized on several populations, including hearing-impaired children is presented.

PICTURE STORY LANGUAGE TEST: The Picture Story Language Test (Myklebust, 1967) is useful in measuring written composition skill of the hearing-impaired child. This standardized test is of particular relevance to a discussion of the elementary-aged, hearing-impaired student, for norms are available for this age group.

The stimulus for the Picture Story Language Test is a single picture about which a child is asked to write a story. The test is scored in three primary ways, productivity, syntactical correctness, and use of abstraction.

The test compares correctness or linguistic structure of a child's production with that of his peers in terms of types of errors, punctuation, substitutions, omissions, additions and word order.

It is useful as a measure of general language functioning in comparison with age peers. It also provides a measure of complexity of language usage from the amount of language produced.

## VOCABULARY MEASUREMENT

Vocabulary is an aspect of language in which many hearing-impaired students often have a deficit. Because of the impact which a deficiency in this area will have on all verbal and academic tasks, vocabulary measurement is being treated separately from other language measurements.

Many elementary-aged, hearing-impaired students have significant vocabulary lags which may be as great as from two to five years below age expectancy. Some lag may be present even when a student appears to have good expressive language skills.

*A relatively cursory evaluation may often give the examiner an erroneously good picture of a student's vocabulary competence. It is important to probe vocabulary concepts in depth to ascertain true competence in this area.*

### Vocabulary Development

During preschool years, the hearing-impaired child should learn most of his new vocabulary in the same manner as his normal hearing peers. But because of his limited ability to hear, he will sometimes miss a part or all spontaneous verbal intonations. During other verbal exchanges, he may perceive only a distorted message. In order to minimize or reduce the possibility of a large vocabulary deficit, because of defective auditory input, special instruction will be needed to help facilitate the child's vocabulary growth.

When the child with normal hearing first enters school, he will probably be able to read and recognize some words which he has been able to use verbally for many years. He begins to associate the verbal words with the written symbol. In contrast, the child with a hearing loss may not yet have acquired the same amount or type of vocabulary. In addition to having to learn sound-symbol association, he will be asked to learn to read words which have not yet become a part of his verbal language repertoire. This is a staggering task to be imposed on a hearing-impaired child. His acquisition of reading skills will subsequently be hampered.

As a student's reading ability increases, he will learn some of his vocabulary through reading. Vocabulary is also steadily increased by television commercials, store-front signs, magazines, toy directions, and other printed items that interest the child. New vocabulary is also learned by the student from the many activities he experiences in his environment.

Because of the hearing-impaired student's limited reading ability, he may acquire proportionately less vocabulary through reading than does his hearing peers. The hearing-impaired student may also increase his vocabulary through television more slowly because he may only hear a part of the message accurately. Items in print may be less meaningful to the hearing-impaired student because he has not distinctly heard discussions about them.

Thus, one can conclude from the aforegoing discussion that a baseline for vocabulary status and development is a necessary starting point with the hearing-impaired student. Chances are great that he will fall well below the vocabulary level of his normal hearing peers.

### Vocabulary Assessment Problems

Vocabulary assessment is complicated by the diversified types of vocabulary used and needed at different grade levels. Yet, a general vocabulary is interspersed in all academic subjects and underlies day to day conversation. Thus, testing must include evaluation of general vocabulary as well as specific subject-area vocabulary. Different methods and tests will be required to measure these two different vocabulary areas.

ASSESSMENT OF GENERAL VOCABULARY: Some standardized tests are available for the measurement of general vocabulary. Vocabulary in standardized tests is usually drawn from words which commonly occur in a reading series. Norms for such general vocabulary tests are usually based on grade equivalency.

One example of a standardized test for measurement of general vocabulary is the World Book Vocabulary Inventory from the World Book Dictionary (Barnhart, 1968). This inventory measures general vocabulary from third grade through college.

As a multiple-choice test, it provides general information about the range of vocabulary capability rather than a fine diagnosis.

Vocabulary measurement is often included as one section of a diagnostic reading test. Reading tests such as the Gates-MacGinitie (Gates, MacGinitie, 1965), the New Developmental Reading Tests (Bond, Balow, Hoyt, 1968), and others, include vocabulary sections.

Separate standardized vocabulary norms are given for each grade level from one through twelve on the Gates-MacGinitie Reading Tests. The student's raw score on the vocabulary portion of the test can be converted into grade and percentile or standard scores by use of an appropriate table of norms. A multiple-choice format with five potential choices is used.

A vocabulary test for intermediate grade levels is included in the New Developmental Reading Tests (Bond, Balow, Hoyt, 1968). The test format is multiple-choice. Comparative grade equivalent norms are available.

Vocabulary subtests from any reading test will meet the requirements of general reading vocabulary testing if they are appropriate to the student's grade and reading level. Careful attention must be given to ascertain whether the child cannot read or does not understand the vocabulary concepts.

While it is helpful for therapy planning purposes to have grade level indicators, vocabulary tests which do not have norms should not be overlooked. Other baseline measures of vocabulary can be used depending upon the needs of a particular student.

ASSESSMENT OF SPECIFIC VOCABULARY: Non-standardized tests are generally the tool used in evaluating specialized subject vocabulary. Special vocabulary is also often assessed by a teacher as one aspect of the student's comprehension of a subject matter area. In other words, vocabulary is measured at the end of a predesignated unit of study by methods deemed appropriate by the teacher.

### MISCELLANEOUS MEASUREMENTS

Three miscellaneous language measurements will be discussed briefly in this section. The first two, organizational skills and ability to understand and follow directions, are non-standardized. The third, achievement tests, has standardized norms. None of these three measurements represent a major means of assessing language functioning. However, all tap aspects of language which are vitally important in the student's day-to-day academic work.

### Informal Tests of Organizational Skills

Success in most life endeavors, and particularly in effective communication, is predicated on the organization of thought and the sequencing of words and ideas. The ability to organize and sequence is needed for language activities which range from writing the letters of the alphabet to composing a term paper. Thus, the hearing-impaired student's organizational skills should be assessed.

The measurement of organizational skills has not been refined to a level which indicates the absolute steps a student should have attained by each grade level. However, if a student with a hearing loss has gross language deficiencies, it is likely that a deficit will also occur in his ability to sequence and organize language.

Sequencing skills of a primary-age child can be assessed by using a picture story with three or four separate scenes. The child is asked to place, in correct order, several pictures which form a sequential story or plot. Depending upon the age of the student, a verbalization of the sequencing activities or the writing of a sequence story might be used for measurement purposes.

By about third grade, a student should be able to arrange four or five major written items in the order of occurrence in a story. Stories similar to those encountered in the student's reading series can be used for this purpose.

A measure similar to the preceding one, but slightly more difficult, is that of having a student choose the correct outline order for a short story. The difficulty level can be increased by the type and amount of material presented. By the mid and late elementary school years, a student should be able to write an outline for a story of three or more paragraphs.

Measures of organization, because of their relative subjectivity, depend upon the skill of the clinician for their interpretation. Their usefulness is dependent upon the needs of the particular student.

### Testing Written Directions

The assessment of a student's ability to understand written directions is vital in determining his performance in certain types of academic skills. A student with normal hearing may have understood all segments of a written direction for many years prior to actually reading and using a direction. But the student with a hearing loss may encounter some of the vocabulary and concepts used in written directions for the very first time. Thus, he may need direct explanation of the vocabulary and concepts used in the directions.

Written directions may be misunderstood for various reasons. Vocabulary may be unknown or unclear to the child. Directions which have two or more parts may be unfamiliar to certain children. The second and third part(s) of multiple-directions may be only partially comprehended and completed by the student. The following sample directions give examples of common error patterns of hard-of-hearing children.

1. A third grade direction: *Underline the correct definition; use the vocabulary word in a sentence.* In this example, the student may not know the meanings of *underline* or *definition* and may neglect to do the second part of the direction.
2. A fourth grade direction: *Number the sentences in the correct order.* The student may not understand the usage of the underlined words *correct order.*
3. A fifth grade direction: *Describe the characteristics of Johnny in the above story.* In this example, the student may not understand the meaning of *describe* or *characteristics.*
4. A sixth grade example: *In each part of the play below, notice the word in parentheses and think how that character sounded, looked and acted as he spoke. Below each conversation, write X before each item that describes something you think he or she did.* The student may not fully comprehend words such as *parentheses, character* or *conversation* and may

become confused if he does not systematically follow each step of the directions.

5. A sixth grade example: *In each statement below, note the relationship between the first two italicized words. Then underline the word that has the same relationship to the third italicized word as the second word has to the first.* The student may have difficulty with vocabulary as well as with comprehension of complex sentence structure.

To determine whether the hearing-impaired student understands written directions, one should ask the student to give verbal definitions and explanations of all vocabulary and sentence structures. He should also be asked to demonstrate his understanding of the directions by working through a practice set of directions.

The use of prepared sets of directions for specific grade levels are valuable in assessing the student's ability to read, understand and follow directions adequately. If prepared or commercial practice sets are not available, an informal judgment of the student's ability to follow directions can be made by checking his ability to follow written directions in his classroom workbooks.

### Achievement Tests

Standardized achievement test scores are generally thought to have some direct relationship to classroom functioning and are usually relatively available in schools. Language subtests of achievement tests are helpful in plotting longitudinal growth of a student. A hearing-impaired student's scores should be compared with and considered within the framework of the range of scores in his classroom to get an adequate idea of his functioning within the class.

The vocabulary subsection can be useful as a pragmatic indicator of the child's general vocabulary functioning. Scores should be interpreted with care. The vocabulary task the student has been expected to do will depend upon the particular achievement test. Although a subtest name may remain essentially the same in a variety of achievement tests, a child may be asked to perform quite different tasks from one test to another. For example, on one vocabulary subtest, a child might be asked to give the phonetic spelling of a given word. On another subtest, he may be asked the definition of a word. In yet another subtest, he may be required to complete a sentence in a multiple-choice manner. Because these tasks are so different, subtest comparison cannot be made from test to test or level to level without a knowledge of what is contained within a particular subtest.

The hearing-impaired student who scores at least six months below grade level, particularly if he is already functioning in the lower half of his class range, has potential problems in the skill area sampled by the achievement tests.

If a student scores significantly below grade level, as indicated above, a scrutiny of subtest items will provide some specific information about skills in which the child is weak. These weak areas thus provide a basis for therapy planning.

### SUMMARY

The acquisition of language skills by hearing-impaired students progresses in a manner similar to that of students with normal hearing. However, those language skills most affected by inadequate auditory input are sometimes acquired more slowly or with greater difficulty by hearing-impaired students.

Such language problems of the hearing-impaired student discussed in this chapter included speech errors, oral language difficulties, written language difficulties, vocabulary deficiencies, difficulties with organizational skills and difficulties in comprehension of written directions.

Formal and informal methods and techniques for evaluating language performance in the probable areas of language difficulty, encountered by the hearing-impaired child, have been described in this chapter. Descriptions included oral language measurement, written language measurement, vocabulary measurement, and three miscellaneous measurements.

By using the methods and techniques of measurements, described in this chapter, a functional profile of language strengths and weaknesses can be obtained. From such a profile, therapy programming for the hearing-impaired student can be structured.

## REFERENCES

Barnhart, C. L. (Ed.): *The World Book Dictionary: A Thorndike-Barnhart Dictionary*. Chicago, Field Enterprises Educational Corporation, 1968.

Bond, G. L., Balow, B., and Hoyt, C.: *New Development Reading Tests Intermediate Level*. Chicago, Lyons and Carnahan, 1968.

Cattell, N. R.: *The New English Grammar: A Descriptive Introduction*. Cambridge, M.I.T. Press, 1969.

Chomsky, C.: *The Acquisition of Syntax in Children from Five to Ten*. Cambridge, M.I.T. Press, Research Monograph No. 57, 1969.

Gates, A. I., and MacGinite, W. H.: *Gates MacGinite Reading Tests*. New York, Teacher's College Press, 1965.

Johnson, W., Darley, F. L., and Spreisterbach, D. C.: *Diagnostic Methods in Speech Pathology*. New York, Harper and Row, 1963.

Myklebust, H. R.: *Development and Disorders of Written Language, Vol. 1, Picture Story Language Test*. New York, Grune & Stratton, 1967.

Streng, A. H.: *Syntax, Speech and Hearing; Applied Linguistics for Teachers of Children with Language and Hearing Disabilities*. New York, Grune & Stratton, 1972.

# CHAPTER VII

# LANGUAGE THERAPY FOR HEARING-IMPAIRED STUDENTS

### Verna Yater and Jackie Simms

THE PLANNING of therapy to nurture the hearing-impaired student's language development is done after assessment. Deficit language areas must be pinpointed before therapy objectives and suitable therapy activities can be established to promote language growth.

Once the student's language needs are identified, therapy planning should be goal oriented and have measurable objectives. It is essential that there be (1) efficiently designed therapy activities to improve a language skill area; (2) accurate assessment of the attainment of the stated therapy goal; and (3) determination of whether the stated goal has been reached within the allotted time.

Therefore, before any therapy suggestions for specific language areas are discussed, the use of global planning (i.e. long range planning), and behavioral objectives (i.e. short term specific planning), will be briefly explained. These two techniques introduce the clinician to planning and management tools which will help him become specific and objective in the attainment of therapy goals.

Specific therapy planning for various areas such as oral language, written language, and vocabulary will also be described and illustrated with sample global plans and behavioral objectives.

### THERAPY PLANNING

Within the confines of a single chapter, it is not possible to discuss all of the factors which the clinician may have to consider in determining a long-range global plan or all the possible

121

short-term behavioral objectives which would eventually lead to the attainment of the therapy goal. Thus, explanations of simplified means and methods of writing global programs as modified from Pipe (1966) and behavioral objectives, Mager (1962) will be presented. These sample global plans and behavioral objectives should be modified to fit the needs of the individual hearing-impaired student.

### Global Planning

A global plan is a general statement of a problem and the goal to be achieved with the student in resolving the problem. For example, *Larry, a fourth grade, ten-year-old, hearing-impaired boy, has language deficits. The language problem includes a vocabulary deficit.*

To help organize global planning, a Global Program Planning and Development Chart is used (see Table 7-I). Included in the chart are columns for *needs, goals, overall evaluation measures,* and *evaluation schedules.*

The *needs* column of the planning chart (Table 7-I, column 1) usually includes four subsections: (1) a description of the student and his grade level; (2) the problem or need area, i.e. vocabulary development or some other language skill area; (3) the pretherapy level of achievement in the specific language area under consideration; and (4) a statement of how the problem area was determined, i.e. information from formal test results, work performance, teacher/clinician observation, etc.

The *goals* section of the planning chart (Table 7-I, column 2) should contain the global plan statement, i.e. the general goal the clinician is attempting to help the student achieve. The approximate type and degree of change to be achieved should also be noted in this column.

*The overall evaluation measures* column of the planning chart (Table 7-I, column 3) is reserved for recording the specific tests and methods that will be used by the clinician in evaluation of the student's progress and eventual achievement of the goal.

*The evaluation schedule* column of the planning chart (Table 7-I, column 4) specifies when pretherapy, therapy progress, and goal achievement testing will be done.

TABLE 7-I

GLOBAL PROGRAM PLANNING AND DEVELOPMENT CHART

| Needs | Goals | Overall Evaluation Measures | Evaluation Schedule |
|---|---|---|---|
| Learner: Larry, eleven year old fourth grade, hearing-impaired student. | To improve student's vocabulary level one-year during the current academic year. | World Book Vocabulary Test, Grade Four. | October, 1972 May, 1973 |
| Area of Need: Vocabulary Development. | | Gates-MacGinitie Reading Test, Vocabulary Sub-Section. | October, 1972 May, 1973 |
| Pretherapy Vocabulary Level: Second grade. | | Clinician-Prepared Tests. EDL Materials. | Pre and post twenty word Learning Units. |
| Source of Determination of Need: World Book Vocabulary Test, 4th Grade Level. | | | |
| Gates-MacGinitie Reading Test, Vocabulary Subsection. | | | |
| Clinician observation of difficulty during therapy session. | | | |
| Teacher reports of classroom work. | | | |

### Behavioral Objectives

Once a global plan has been written for a specific language area, behavioral objectives or specific steps of therapy are written to help to achieve the goal of the global plan. One or more behavioral objectives will be necessary to attain the final therapy goal, i.e. completion of the global plan.

Basically, a behavioral objective is a statement of (a) the specific task the student is to do within a restricted set of circumstances, (b) the level of skill he is to attain in doing it, and (c) the amount of time which will be allowed for reaching the goal.

The following steps in writing behavioral objectives have been outlined by Mager (1962).

1. *The initial statement is simply who will be influenced or changed during the learning.* For example, the student will be able to. . . . John will be able to. . . .
2. *Identify specifically what the student will be doing by using an action or behavioral verb.* These should indicate exactly what the student will be doing. For example, *recite, list, write, match, cut, report,* are behavioral verbs because they indicate a very specific activity. Verbs such as *learn, comprehend* or *understand* are not acceptable behavioral verbs. They do not indicate in a specifically observable manner what a student is expected to do.
3. *Indicate under what conditions or restrictions behavior will occur.* For example, *in each of three paragraphs* is a restriction. *While reading orally* is a restriction or condition.
4. *Indicate the acceptable level of performance which represents the student's achievement of the goal, that is, the criterion level.* For example, *with eighty-five percent accuracy* or *with only one error.*
5. *Indicate the time period in which the criterion level will be reached.* For example, *within three twenty-minute therapy sessions,* or *after fifteen minutes of practice.*

Some examples of behavioral objectives are listed below. The numbers above each portion of the behavioral objective represents the steps in writing an objective as given above.

(1)                                   (2)
*/The child will be able to/  find and underline/  the topic sentence*
(3)                                   (4)
*in each of three paragraphs/  with one hundred percent accuracy/*
(5)
*after training in two therapy sessions.*
(1)                                   (2)
*/Billy will be able to/  match meanings with words/  from the*
(3)
*first story in the Scott Foresman's Grade Three basal reader/  to a*
(4)                                   (5)
*level of thirteen out of fifteen correct/  within two therapy sessions./*

In order to assess whether a student has reached a behavioral objective, test(s) should be given to him. The posttherapy test should be an indicator of therapy success, i.e. whether or not the therapy objective has been achieved.

## ORAL LANGUAGE THERAPY

Four areas of oral language difficulties frequently encountered by the hearing-impaired student could be described as (1) verbal language errors, (2) speech errors, (3) question form errors, and (4) syntactical errors. Each of these problem areas will be considered in the following section with therapy suggestions for their resolution.

### *Verbal Language Errors*

The hearing-impaired student who has difficulty in the area of oral language expression will need practice in expressing himself orally. For example, the student might be asked to describe objects, to talk about pictures, to explain the steps in a game, to describe a section of his classroom or to talk about any meaningful activities surrounding him. Full expansion of his oral language and correct language modeling should always be provided for the child.

A behavioral objective to improve the general verbal language of a hearing-impaired kindergarten or first grade child might be written as follows:

> *Bob will be able to verbally describe, in complete sentences, ten simple object pictures with no errors after two therapy sessions.*

The clinician would have already determined that Bob did not use complete sentences when speaking about these pictures. Activities employed to reach the objective might include the following:

1. The clinician contrasts naming and listing responses with complete sentences while discussing objects in the therapy room.
2. The clinician makes comments about objects in the room. He has the child hold up a puppet, called Mr. Sentence, if the clinician's statement was a complete sentence.
3. The child is encouraged to discuss objects in the therapy room. He is told to use complete sentences when Mr. Sentence, controlled by the clinician, pops from behind a partitition. Mr. Sentence will ask questions to elicit complete responses and will provide any expansion or correction of the child's verbalizations. Mr. Sentence asks the child to repeat the corrected or expanded responses. The clinician verbally reinforces the child's correct responses.
4. Mr. Sentence shows the child ten pictures, asking him to describe the pictures. Mr. Sentence will comment and ask questions about the pictures, such as, *Tell me about this picture,* or *What color is the kite?* Mr. Sentence will provide any expansion or correction needed.
5. A posttherapy test is given in which the child is asked to verbally describe each picture with a sentence statement.

The effectiveness with which the therapy objective will be reached will depend, in part, upon the reinforcement parents and classroom teachers offer the child.

### Speech Errors

The hearing-impaired student may misuse inflectional suffixes and noun-plural affixes because of speech misarticulations and omissions. The most frequently deleted inflectional suffixes are the /s/, /es/, /z/ or /ez/ ordinarily added to nouns to form plurals; the /s/ ordinarily added to a verb stem to form the third person singular of the present tense; the /ed/ or /t/ ordinarily added to a verb to form the past tense; and the /'s/ or /s'/ ordinarily added to nouns to show possession.

To help make the student aware of his errors, he should be given many opportunities to see when and how he is deleting endings and what effect these errors have on the meaning and usage of language. This can be done by writing out specific rules such as *the /ed/ added to a verb signifies past tense* or write */s/ or /es/ added to a noun forms a plural.* These examples can also be put on flash cards which will help to serve as a reminder for the student.

Indicators of plural usage such as *some, dozens of, many* and *a few* can also serve to alert the student to the proper use of plurals. These clues, too, can be put on flash cards or into notebooks for the students' ready reference. Such examples should include phrases such as *some balloons, dozens of flowers, many quarters,* or *a few cookies.*

If the child's oral language gives indications of language related speech errors, direct teaching of deficit areas should be undertaken. Even with inadequate auditory input, students can learn to use language structure correctly.

### Question Form Usage Errors

Most question forms are used correctly, at least orally, by children with normal hearing by the time they enter first grade. The child with a hearing loss is still often unable to use question forms correctly by first grade level. Thus, a hearing-impaired student who exhibits errors in the use of question forms will need specific instruction in this area.

Using question forms correctly requires that the student understand the meanings of the frequently used question referents, i.e. *what, who, where, when, why* and *how.* He must also understand the concept of transposition, i.e. transformation of the syntactical structure involved in movement from a statement to a question. In addition, he needs to understand the concepts of space, time, and causality.

It is useful for the child to know that the *wh questions* relate to only one part of a sentence. Simple explanations to the stu-

TABLE 7-II

GLOBAL PROGRAM PLANNING AND DEVELOPMENT CHART

| Needs | Goals | Overall Activities | Evaluation Measures | Evaluation Schedule |
|---|---|---|---|---|
| Learner: Charis, A ten year old, fourth grade student. Area of Need: Language, Question Form Usage. Source of Determination of Need: Informal written and oral question form. | To improve Charis' knowledge of when to use specific questions and how to correctly ask the questions. | Same as the first activity in the evaluation measure section of this chart but with a visual aid card with "what kind of . . ." written on it and some clinician assistance. Clinician asks Charis several "What kind of" questions. Ex: "What kind of cereal did you have for breakfast? What kind of candy do you like? What kind object do you have in your room?" Look around therapy room. Count the number of "what kind of" questions the clinician and Charis can think of. Ex: "What kind of pencil do you have? What kind of clothing do you have on? What kind of book is on the table? What kind | Prior to starting activities— "I am thinking of an object game. Charis can ask three questions to determine what the object is, then guess. The first question must be "What kind of object is it?" "What did I bring?" game Charis can ask three questions to determine what was brought, then guess. The first question must be a "what kind of" question. Ex: Clinician says, "I brought an object with me today." Half the objects will be tested orally and for the other half Charis will write the question. | 10/29/71 11/15/71 |

of jewelry do you have on?"

Charis is given a list of nouns. Ex: Dresses, shoes, ice cream for which she must ask the clinician a "what kind of" question.

Clinician thinks of a category name. Ex: Meat, furniture, desserts, vegetable, fruits, school, then gives clues about it. Ex: "I am thinking about something to eat. It is the flesh of animals." This is followed by a "what kind of" question which Charis should, by then, be able to answer. Ex: "What kind of food is it?"

Charis is given a list of several category names and told to pick one (at a time) to give clues on. Charis plays the role of the clinician in activity number 4 listed above.

Behavioral Objective: Charis will be able to appropriately ask a "what kind of" question, both in verbal and written form when trying to guess what the clinician brought or is thinking of with one hundred percent accuracy in two weeks with ten minute therapy sessions, three times per week.

dent regarding these concepts are helpful. Explaining relationships such as *what indicates objects; who indicates people; where signifies places; when indicates time; why means because of;* and *how means in some way.* Keeping such explanations on flash cards for reinforcement while explaining and reviewing question forms will be useful.

Activities, situations, and motivational devices are needed to provide experience for the student in using question forms correctly. A simple technique which can be used for such development is that of saying or writing answers to which the child has to formulate appropriate questions. For example, the clinician might write, *I have two red flowers.* The child would then say or write a question similar to, *How many red flowers do you have? What colors are your flowers?* or *What do you have?*

Table 7-II shows a sample global program plan for improvement of a fourth grade, hearing-impaired girl's verbal question form usage. This chart is a variation of the global planning chart, previously seen, in that the behavioral objective is found at the bottom of the chart and the activities to achieve the behavioral objective are written in the overall activities section of the chart.

The following is a transcription of a portion of the first therapy session which was based on the initial activity listed in the global planning chart (Table 7-II, column 3).

> Clinician:   Today we're going to play a guessing game, but it's different from other guessing games we've played. You may ask only three questions. The special question for today is a "what kind of" question. (Clinician places the card with the words, "What kind of . . ." written on it in front of the child.) That's the question you have to ask first. Then you'll find out what kind of thing it is, and you can ask any other two questions, and then guess what I'm thinking about. For example, I will say, "I am thinking about an object." Your first question should be, "What kind of object is it?"
>
> Charis: What kind of object is it?
>
> Clinician: And I would say, "It is a piece of furniture." Then you would have two more questions to ask me. Do you want to try to finish this one?
>
> Charis: Yes.

Clinician: Ok, you have two more questions, then you guess.

Charis: Umm . . . mm. What . . . umm.

Clinician: I don't care; anything at all that you want to ask.

Charis: Even a color?

Clinician: Anything, I don't care. Any question at all. Anything that you think will help you guess what I'm thinking about.

Charis: Ok. What color is it?

Clinician: It can be many different colors.

Charis: Does it has, does it has four squares?

Clinician: What?

Charis: Does it has four squares?

Clinician: Does it have four squares? I don't know what you mean by that.

Charis: Well, does it has?

Clinician: Does it have.

Charis: Four squares?

Clinician: What do you mean four squares?

Charis: I mean four—you know; here's a corner, there's a corner, there's a corner.

Clinician: You mean, is it a square? Does it have four corners?

Charis: Yeah.

Clinician: Ok. Well kind of. If you look at the whole thing it usually looks oblong, like a rectangle.

Charis: Is it a couch?

Clinician: Right! How did you guess that?

Charis: Well, 'cause you told me it was a triangle.

Clinician: Not a triangle.

Charis: No, it looks like a triangle.

Clinician: Not like a triangle. What did I say?

Charis: A rectangle?

Clinician: Rectangle! Yes, a rectangle has four sides. A triangle has
. . .

Charis: Three!

Clinician: Three. I didn't say triangle. You're right; you guessed it. You understand the game now?

Charis: Yeah.

Clinician: Ok. I want you to try to ask good questions. And remember, the first one has to be a "what kind of" question. Let's see if we can try another one.

Charis: Another object?

Clinician: I am thinking of another object.

Charis: What kind of object is it?

Clinician: It is a beverage. Do you know that word—beverage?

Charis: No.

Clinician: Beverage means something that you drink.
Charis: What kind of, what kind is it?
Clinician: I already told you what kind of thing or object it is and I'm not going to tell you what kind of beverage it is. You have to guess that. You have to ask a different question now.
Charis: What color is the drink?
Clinician: It's white. . . . Do you want to ask another question? You have one more question to ask, then you can guess.
Charis: I know what the answer is.
Clinician: Well, ask another question and be sure.
Charis: Umm, let's see. Do babies drink it?
Clinician: Yes. Ok, you asked all of your questions. Guess.
Charis: Is it milk?
Clinician: It's milk, right.

Other objects and categories used for this lesson were apples (fruit), hamburger (meat), and dahlias (flower).

The student illustrated in this therapy lesson had been attempting to use the *what kind of* question form and understood its meaning, but she had difficulty combining the words in a grammatically correct manner. Although Charis had reasonable success with the use of the question form in this lesson, the other activities using this question form (noted in Table 7-II) should not be omitted. They are needed for reinforcement and for presenting examples of the many instances in which this type of question may be asked.

Other approaches and activities for question form therapy are dependent upon the abilities of the child and the particular type of question form being developed. Carol Chomsky (1969) suggests some avenues for testing question form use. Clinicians working with hearing-impaired students may find it beneficial to explore her basic techniques and to revise or adapt them for therapy use. An excellent explanation of question form development is also offered by Streng (1972).

### Syntactical Errors

Some hearing-impaired students appear to have what can most graphically be described as *scrambled* verbal language. A child whose verbal language is scrambled, or syntactically incorrect, might say *I went to the movie with my friend of mine.* For this and other types of sequential ordering errors, the clinician may utilize auditory and visual patterning to help build acceptable sentence structure.

Auditory patterning, i.e. verbal correction and/or expansion of what the student says, should be used consistently by the clinician. Oral language patterning should be done spontaneously as incorrect language is produced as well as on a preplanned basis.

If the child is experiencing little growth in correct oral language production by use of oral-auditory patterning, visual (written) patterning should be utilized in conjunction with the auditory patterning. The following is a behavioral objective for correction of syntactically incorrect oral language order with written (visual) patterning aids.

> *Fred will be able to say in elliptical sentences, which are chosen by the clinician, the phrases "a friend of mine," "my friend," "a friend" and "my friend John" with no errors in two therapy sessions.*

The clinician could first use the following pattern: *(who) (verb) (where or what) with a friend of mine.*

Activities using this pattern might be as follows:

1. The child would be shown that his original sentence, *I went to a movie with my friend of mine,* could be corrected using a pattern. The particular pattern should have been written on a piece of sentence strip or some sturdy paper and posted in a place which is easy to see and reach.
2. Individual cards with the following words written on them would be used: The subject word, *I,* the verb, *went,* several different *where phrases* (i.e. *to a movie, to the dime store, to school*), the preposition, *with* and the phrase, *a friend of mine.* The student would place the cards in the order of the visual pattern to make various statements. For this activity, all the cards would remain constant except the *where* card. For example:
   (I) (went) (to Grant's Farm) (with) (a friend of mine.)
   (I) (went) (to the hockey game) (with) (a friend of mine.)

Note how the *where* slot changed including *to Grant's Farm* and *to the hockey game* while all others did not change. The student would say each sentence aloud as he completed it.

3. This activity is similar to the above; however, the student now would also have a choice of subject cards. For example, he might now use:

> (Tom) (went) (to the principal's office) (with) (a friend of mine.)
>
> (Bill and I) (went) (to the basketball practice) (with) (a friend of mine.)

4. Different verb and object cards are now added. The only cards remaining constant are *with* and *a friend of mine;* sentences which the child might produce are:

> (I) (ate) (ice cream) (with) (a friend of mine.)
>
> (Harry and I) (played) (baseball) (with) (a friend of mine.)

5. The alternate prepositions *to* and *for* are added to the pattern. Cards made for the *to* or *for* cards could be exchanged for the *with* card. The child might formulate sentences such as:

> (I) (gave) (my kite) (to) (a friend of mine.)
>
> (Mother) (bought) (a toy car) (for) (a friend of mine.)

In each of these activities the *a friend of mine* card has remained constant, and the child has said aloud each sentence he made with the cards. The substitutes, *a friend, my friend,* and *my friend John,* will be introduced one at a time and only after each usage is thoroughly mastered.

The clinician may find the use of the above described patterning helpful for correcting syntactical errors. However, caution is advised against the constant use of patterns as a yardstick for measuring and building a child's language so as not to stifle language creativity and stultify the child's verbalizations.

## WRITTEN LANGUAGE THERAPY

In considering specific suggestions for improving the hearing-impaired student's written language, the clinician should begin the student's writing tasks at the level which he can accomplish adequately. The student's writing skills may initially be so poor that he will have to dictate and the clinician do the writing. Another student may be able to produce only poorly constructed sentences. He may need help in writing one sentence at a time with correction and expansion offered by the clinician.

Many hearing-impaired students will initially have simple, immature writing styles because of low vocabulary levels and inexperience with usage of varied language structures. These students will need opportunities to use figurative language, to learn multiple meanings of words and to practice saying and writing things in different ways.

The following writing experiences will be beneficial to hearing-impaired students who function at different levels of written language.

1. Provide sentences or paragraphs with blanks, and let the student complete them. This should be a beginning experience only to correspond with the clinician's oral expansion. This kind of exercise is a visual language experience. It is not growth-producing when a child begins to be capable of his own written language production.
2. Provide the student with sentence beginnings and ask him to complete them. Any correct completion is accepted. This is the beginning of incomplete sentence generation by the student and will only be needed if he has great difficulty spontaneously generating language.
3. Let the student tell you a story and then have him write it from key phrases and words you have written for him from his oral story.
4. Ask the student to construct complete sentences from interchangeable noun, verb and auxiliary phrases written on cards or paper strips. The complexity of the phrases should be geared to the student's written language functioning level.
5. Ask the student to describe objects in a room, parts of a room, a game or other items in his immediate vicinity. The description should include properties of the subject such as size, shape, weight, etc.
6. Ask the student to caption newspaper pictures, to write scripts for cartoons, or to write newspaper articles.

The following is a Global Program Plan; it includes behavioral objective and selected segments of a transcribed sample therapy session in the area of written language for a fifth grade hearing-impaired student attending a regular school. As seen in the Global Program Plan, Table 7-III, the child was receiving individual therapy as well as instruction in language skill areas in his regular classroom program.

A behavioral objective in the development of written language was written as follows:

*Paul will be able to write a story of at least six sentences which, in its corrected form, will be correct in terms of syntax and structure by the end of two, thirty minute therapy sessions.*

Activities:

1. The clinician will explain the task to Paul.
2. The clinician will allow Paul to choose one of three pictures to use in the therapy session.
3. Paul will tell a verbal story about the picture.
4. The clinician and Paul will expand the story; the clinician will teach new vocabulary concepts.
5. The clinician will summarize the newly expanded story at several intervals.
6. After expansion, Paul will again tell a verbal story about the picture.
7. Paul will be given sentence strips and asked to write one sentence of his story per sentence strip.
8. Paul will be asked to give his story a title.
9. Paul and the clinician will correct each sentence he has written; oral and written corrections will be made.
10. After each sentence has been corrected on the sentence strip, Paul will rewrite the complete corrected story on paper.
11. Paul and the clinician will double check his completely rewritten story; this will be done by reading it orally and making minute corrections.

Evaluation: Judgment of acceptable standards of syntax and structure will be made by the clinician along with the child.

Segments of the therapy session included herein are as follows: (1) the clinician's explanation of the task, (2) the stu-

TABLE 7-III

GLOBAL PROGRAM PLANNING AND DEVELOPMENT CHART

| Needs | Goal | Activities | Evaluation Measure | Evaluation Schedule |
|---|---|---|---|---|
| **Learner:** Paul a fifth grade student. | To improve the student's ability to write story material. | Verbalizing material to increase vocabulary concepts and ability to structure. | Clinician and child judgement of correctness of production. | Done as each writing exercise is completed. |
| **Area of Need:** Written Language. | | Practice with structural parts to increase child's ability to maneuver statements both verbal and written. | Error Analysis Chart. | Each month November, 1971 through May, 1972. |
| **Source of Determination of Need:** Observations of work in therapy and from child's classroom. | | Teaching of parts of speech to improve correct usage. Practice with talking and writing in natural patterns and immediate straightening. | | |

dent's original verbal story, (3) selected portions of the verbal expansion and explanation process, (4) the student's verbal story after verbal expansion by the clinician, (5) the student's original written story, and (6) his final written story. (See Figure 7-1 for the picture stimulus for this therapy session.)

1. Clinician's Explanation of the Task:

> Paul, you have a picture in front of you. You will write a story about the picture. Before you write the story, I'd like you to talk about it, then you'll write your story on strips of paper and we'll rewrite it. First, tell me a little about what you are going to write.

2. Student's Original Verbal Story:

> One day they went on a hike and early in the morning there had been a little bit of drizzling and it went on the phone, all of the Cub Scouts crowded and crushing in there and they all know the way they are going and it's pouring down there and then when it's finally stopped that he hung the telephones that he went out.

After this initial verbal story was given by the child, he was

Figure 7-1. Motivational picture used for student's written story.

guided into organizing his story material. His ideas were strengthened and vocabulary explanations were provided. Note in the following text some expansion of concepts and vocabulary explanation. Notice also that the clinician attempts to draw the vocabulary from the child rather than simply providing the correct word. In this segment, at one point, the child attempts to avoid or circumvent a word he does not know, not uncommon for a child with vocabulary deficits but who has a fair degree of language facility.

3. Selected Portions of the Verbal Expansion and Explanation Process:

Clinician: Ok, Paul, that's pretty good; you have some good ideas there. Let's talk about them some more. We see the Cub Scouts on the picture. Where are the Cub Scouts?

Paul: In the telephone.

Clinician: In the telephone?

Paul: No, in the telephone place to talk.

Clinician: What do you call that telephone place to talk?

Paul: I don't know.

Clinician: It's called the telephone—what?

Paul: Do—, I don't know.

Clinician: Are we in a telephone—whatever that is?

Paul: Talk?

Clinician: No. You go into the telephone — to talk, but what's the name of it? A telephone—?

Paul: Case?

Clinician: It's like a case. It's like a case, but there's a special name for it.

Paul: I don't know.

Clinician: All the Scouts are in the telephone booth. A telephone booth. Have you used a telephone booth?

Paul: No.

Clinician: No? Have you seen a telephone booth outside of this picture?

Paul: Yeah.

Clinician: Where have you seen a telephone booth?

Paul: Right by, around store, across down there.

Clinician: Right across from where?

Paul: Uh, Sappington Street.

Clinician: Sappington Street, right across from your what?

Paul: School.

Clinician: Right across from the school there's a what?

Paul: Store.

Clinician: And what's in front of the store?

Paul: The telephone booth.

Clinician: A telephone booth. Ok. Is that the only place you've ever seen a telephone booth?

Paul: Couple more things, couple more place.

Clinician: A couple more places? You've seen it in a few more places?

Paul: Uh huh.

Clinician: Where else have you seen a telephone booth?

Paul: In the parking lot.

Clinician: Where in the parking lot?

Paul: I don't know.

Clinician: Oh, you mean in some parking lot?

Paul: Uh huh.

Clinician: You've seen a telephone booth in some parking lots? Could you have seen a telephone booth when you went to the ball game?

Paul: Yeah.

In the above example the clinician first tried to draw out the child's concept of telephone booth and then attempted to re-iterate the term *booth* frequently. Next is an example of resummarizing and organizing for the student.

Clinician: A telephone booth, right. Ok. So we have the Scouts in a telephone booth.

Here is a second summary of the child's story by the clinician, after several more minutes of expansion and explanation.

Clinician: We have the Scouts and the Scoutmaster in the telephone booth, with a road map, making a telephone call to another Scoutmaster. The Scoutmaster is asking him to send a car. Is that correct? Ok. Tell me now how you think you might write this story. Let's summarize it.

4. Student's Verbal Story After Verbal Expansion by the Clinician:

Paul: And suddenly they had a little drizzle, they didn't go inside the telephone booth, yeah, pretty soon it rains harder, they kept walking, they couldn't find any yet, awhile they found a telephone booth, they came right in there and the Scoutmaster called to another Scoutmaster, so he said, "Where are we?" and he said,

"Where are you? Tell me a clue." Then he said, "We're right next to Highway 66 and would you pick a car for us, take us home?" and he said, "Ok, goodbye." Then he came to there and then it stopped, then it was too late, then he came when it stopped rain.
Clinician: Ok.
Paul: And then he went back home, the car and the Scout didn't go yet. They didn't go. They still kept going on a hike, then the same thing happens again and he calls again in telephone booth. That's about it.
Clinician: Ok, now, let's begin to write the story. We'll do one sentence at a time. How would that be?

The child then wrote each sentence on a strip of paper. Corrections were not made at this point. The child's initial written sentences, without corrections, are reproduced below. Slashes are used to indicate the end of each thought.

5. Student's Original Written Story:

One day the cubscout went on a hiking and it was dristly. They drazy/ They ... ... hiking all away to the telephone booth./ The Scoutmaster talk ... telephone and he said, We are on Highway 66. Then another man said went to get his car bring/ The car came and then the rain stop that was strange / The car went back home and the Scout ... didn't go in the car./ The it start ... raining again./ They went back the Telephone booth./

The student was asked to first verbalize the sentences he would write. In no case did he write what he had stated, his verbal statements were as would be expected, more complex than his written sentences. As the student wrote each sentence, no corrections were made. During the next therapy session, the student was asked to correct one sentence at a time. The clinician explained and suggested but allowed the child to correct the sentences in the manner in which he wanted to, i.e. in the form he preferred to use. After correction, the following is the child's final written story.

6. Student's Final Written Story:

One day, the Cub Scouts went on a hike. It was drizzling. They hiked to the telephone booth. The Scoutmaster talked on the telephone and he said, "We are on Highway 66." Then another man said, "I will bring my car." The car came and then the rain stopped; that was strange. The car went back home and the Scouts didn't go in the car. Then it started raining again. They went back to the telephone booth.

As seen in the story above, this student successfully attained the objective of having written a story of at least six sentences which, in its corrected form, according to general use measures, is correct in terms of syntax and structure. This goal was accomplished by the end of two thirty minute therapy sessions.

Other source material for written work appears in the appendix.

## VOCABULARY ACQUISITION

Many students with a hearing loss will have a vocabulary deficiency. Diagnostic probing may have uncovered a general vocabulary deficit or deficits only in certain academic areas. In either case, programming for vocabulary therapy should include verbal stimulation and reading.

### Verbal Stimulation for Vocabulary Building

The hearing-impaired student needs the verbal stimulation of hearing words, having their meanings explained and producing them verbally again and again.

An excellent and natural way for the very young school-aged, hard-of-hearing child to learn vocabulary is to be bombarded with verbal stimuli. Just as in the preschool years, it is initially important for the child to hear repeated explanations and repetitions of rhythm and meaning as outlined by Van Riper (1950); so too, the primary-aged child needs this type of verbal stimulation. The hard-of-hearing child needs to hear something, hear it again and hear it once more for reiteration.

A behavioral objective based on the concept of verbal stimulation for vocabulary development for the first grade child might, for example, read as follows:

*Peter will be able to verbally identify from a picture notebook made from collected magazine pictures or live drawings, twelve sports activities with no errors after three therapy sessions.*

The clinician will have determined by using a picture dictionary that the child did not know about the twelve pictures prior to the beginning of therapy.

Activities will include:

1. The mounting of sports activity pictures into a notebook while child and clinician talk about them.
2. The clinician will explain each picture so that she frequently reiterates the name of the sports activity. For example she might say: *table tennis. The two girls are playing table tennis. Have you ever played table tennis? Usually two people play table tennis. Sometimes four people play table tennis. They call it playing doubles. The table they use for table tennis is always the same size. Some people call table tennis ping-pong. Sometimes people play table tennis in their basements.*
3. As a picture is mounted, the child will indicate which sports activity is represented, i.e., skating, skiing, table tennis, etc.
4. After each picture has been placed into a notebook, the clinician again repeats the name of the sports activity.
5. The child is then asked to discuss some aspects of the sports activity.
6. A post-test is given in which the child is asked to verbally identify each of the twelve sports activities.

While the above activities are being used in therapy, parents should be encouraged to explain, expand, refine and upgrade the child's differentiation of sports related objects and ideas surrounding him. His peers and classroom teacher should be encouraged to do so too.

It is important, for example, in the home to talk about sports, foods, autos, airplanes, etc. in specific extended terms rather than general ones. For example, food should be discussed as *pie crust, chocolate malt, seasoning, two percent,* etc., instead of merely *a top for the pie, something to drink, salt and pepper,* or *milk.* Cars might include *Volvos, Fords, Chevies, Chryslers,* etc., as well as finer differentiations such as *Bonneville, LeSabre, hardtop,* etc.

In addition to the many repetitions needed by the hard-of-hearing student, some feedback from him is needed to check the accuracy of his perception. For example, if a student says that *mini* means a *lot of,* the clinician needs to be aware that this student has perceived the word as *many,* a word he already knew.

Also, *logs* might, for example, be perceived by the child with a hearing loss as *dogs*. This misperception might help explain his perplexity at being asked whether he likes to eat *logs*. Even perceiving *logs* as *logs* might cause some confusion in understanding if he has not been exposed to *logs* as a variation of a sweet roll.

Words or sentences requiring the attachment of meaning to an auditory event may need direct explanation. Such concepts as a *whisper, dead silence,* or *the rustle of leaves* may require direct explanation. The student's classroom teachers, peers and family need to be made aware of the student's possible confusions.

### *Vocabulary Acquisition from Reading*

By the second or third grade level most students with normal hearing are rapidly accumulating concepts from reading although still learning a great deal of vocabulary from verbal stimulation. Students with hearing loss will often not have acquired reading skills as good as those of their hearing peers and will, therefore, often acquire limited, new vocabulary from reading. Thus direct, concentrated vocabulary instruction is necessary for the hearing-impaired student.

Direct vocabulary instruction can be conducted by use of Educational Development Laboratories (EDL) Core Vocabulary (Taylor and Frackenpohl, 1960). Since the EDL Core Vocabulary has been taken from nine basal reading series, the vocabulary which is used for each grade level can be expected to be frequently encountered by the student in classroom reading. Written exercises are used with this material in conjunction with and following verbal explanations by a clinician. Pretherapy and posttherapy tests have also been devised for segments of the vocabulary material.

Direct vocabulary instruction can also be done for the materials that a child might need to learn at a particular grade level. For example, if, from testing, it was found that the child has deficits in certain academic categories such as science or history, vocabulary concepts pertinent to these skill areas may be taught in a direct manner. Vocabulary contained in specific subject matter areas can be introduced to the student in advance of his class-room work and reinforced by both his classroom teachers and the clinician.

Vocabulary acquisition can be reinforced in the classroom, in therapy sessions, and at home by various means. For example, review on flash cards can be made. These cards should have a word or phrase on one side and its meaning on the other. These words or phrases might also be color-coded, by parts of speech. Later, the student can be encouraged to use the colored cards as the basis for sentence patterning.

Devices, such as a game of concentration with ten definition cards exposed and ten word cards turned word down are often motivational. The child's task is to turn up word cards until he finds one word card to correctly match a definition card.

Other techniques which may be used to motivate the student to learn vocabulary are as follows:

1. Motivational devices in the classroom are *two barrels*, one for vocabulary words and the other for definition cards. The hearing-impaired child and his classmates can draw a word card and then take three turns trying to find the meaning card. Cards in the barrel might be changed about once a week by an appointed child or the teacher.
2. A variation of a *spell down* is still another motivator. A word is given to a student and he is asked to verbally explain its meaning; if he cannot do so he is out of the game. This activity continues until only one player remains.
3. Any recording device can be used as a modified teaching machine; particularly useful are those with cards as well as tapes. A vocabulary word is written on the front of a card; two repetitions of the word are recorded on tape. The student, after listening to the vocabulary word, records the meaning to be checked later by clinician or teacher.
4. New vocabulary should be posted in a child-oriented manner on home and school bulletin boards. Words and their meanings can be put on various designs such as footballs, balloons, dogs, stick figures, or others to maintain the child's interest.

Class and family members should attempt to use new vocabulary words to reinforce their retention.

## *Vocabulary of Current Events*

The enhancement of vocabulary from current events is important. Current events are often discussed and analyzed in the classroom during the middle and upper grades. By the middle grades, there appears to be an increased interest among children in the understanding of current social problems. This interest may be stimulated by social studies texts and teacher materials.

Without specific instruction, many hearing-impaired students are unfamiliar with vocabulary from current events. Since they often miss or misperceive current vocabulary from radio or television, their first exposure to it may come by way of the written word.

To teach the hearing-impaired student new vocabulary concepts from current events, newspapers are the most commonly used printed material. Newspapers are valuable because they introduce new vocabulary in context, usually do not develop an inordinate number of new words per article, and have timely topics.

Many regular city newspapers publish an educational weekly which contains a summary of the week's news. Student newspapers also serve as highly motivating and pertinent sources of new vocabulary geared to specific reading levels. High-interest, low-reading level newspapers such as *You and Your World* and *Know Your World* (Lane, 1972) have varied interest articles as well as regular cartoons, fiction and study sections. They can also be used for recreational reading and as discussion material with parents and peers.

Various other source material and ideas for use in vocabulary development can be found in the appendix. Materials for development of reading skills are also presented in the appendix.

### SUMMARY

Planning for language development was discussed in terms of goals and behavioral objectives. Goals and objectives were defined; steps in planning and writing them were explained. Therapy planning suggestions for some common areas of language difficulties were offered. Specifically discussed were language problems related to speech errors, question form usage, word order and general oral language, written language, and vocabulary development. Therapy planning discussions were supplemented in each section by illustrated behavioral objectives.

## REFERENCES

Chomsky, C.: *The Acquisition of Syntax in Children from Five to Ten.* Cambridge, M.I.T. Press, Research Monograph No. 57, 1969.

Lane, K. (Ed.): *Know Your World.* Columbus, American Education Publications, 1972.

Lane, K. (Ed.): *You and Your World.* Columbus, American Education Publications, 1972.

Mager, R. F.: *Preparing Instructional Objectives.* Belmont, Fearon Publishers, 1962.

Pipe, P.: *Practical Programming.* New York, Holt, Rinehart and Winston, 1966.

Streng, A. H.: *Syntax, Speech and Hearing; Applied Linguistics for Teachers of Children with Language and Hearing Disabilities.* New York, Grune and Stratton, 1972.

Taylor, S. E. and Frackenpohl, H.: *A Core Vocabulary.* Huntington, Educational Developmental Laboratories, 1960.

Van Riper, C.: *Teaching Your Child to Talk.* New York, Harper and Row, 1950.

# CHAPTER VIII

# AUDITORY TRAINING AND SPEECHREADING: SUGGESTIONS FOR THE CLINICIAN

## ROLLIE R. HOUCHINS

LARGE NUMBERS of school-age, hearing-impaired children remain in a regular school without sufficient supportive help from programs providing auditory training and speechreading. The purpose of this chapter, then, is to discuss the management problems related to the acquisition and improvement of auditory and visual perceptual skills and to suggest procedures associated with remediation in auditory training and speechreading.

### THE PROBLEM

The hearing-impaired student is expected to make many adjustments regarding his placement in a regular classroom. Because he may be one of twenty-five to thirty students, the regular classroom teacher is often unable to provide an optimal communication setting or initiate activities which would be supportive to his growth in receptive language.

The hearing-impaired child will discover that because of his hearing deficit, the interpretation of distorted auditory signals can result in misunderstanding. Therefore, it is imperative that he learn how to interpret sound in the presence of this distortion.

The student must also become aware of the numerous and varied visual cues from which he may be able to gain meaning from the visual stimulus and accompanying context. Due to the similarity of innumerable visual clues from the lips, he must be taught to utilize the process of elimination, environmental clues, or other clues which could partially reveal the essence of the message.

148

## EVALUATING THE PROBLEM

The extent of the habilitation or remediation program will be determined for each individual based on the information concerned with (a) the etiology of the hearing loss, (b) age of the student at onset of the loss, (c) severity of the hearing loss, (d) social and psychological information, (e) educational level, and (f) the family's ability to assist in an educational program.

### Etiology

Whenever possible, it is useful to know the cause of the hearing loss. Such knowledge will aid the clinician in becoming aware of and understanding many of the learning and language problems that may be directly or indirectly related to the hearing loss. For example, post-rubella youngsters may have visual impairments or learning problems, as well as a language deficit caused by the hearing loss.

When hearing loss occurs, after some language has been acquired, the problem which caused the hearing loss could also be responsible for other physiological and psychological problems. An example of this might be the child who has had meningitis.

### Age of Onset

The age at which the hearing loss occurred is important datum for the clinician to know. This information could contribute additional diagnostic facts relative to the level of linguistic functioning, for it is reasonably clear that the longer a child is exposed to normal auditory inputs for speech and language, the better his linguistic skills.

### Severity of the Loss

It is common knowledge, with other things being equal, that a child born with a ninety dB loss, through the speech frequency range, has a greater detriment to his development of speech and language than a child with a forty-five dB loss.

The audiometric configuration (shape of the pure-tone audiometric curve) provides some insight and understanding as to how individuals with defective mechanisms use, or may learn to use, their hearing. For example, amplification is most often useful to the student who has a relatively flat, bilaterally symmetrical, pure-tone audiometric configuration. In general, the more the pure-tone curve deviates from this pattern, the more difficulty the hearing-impaired individual may experience in auditory discrimination of conversational speech.

### Social and Emotional Factors

In order to benefit most from auditory training and speech-reading instruction, or for that matter, any educational instruction, the youngster should be comfortable socially as well as emotionally.

When hearing-impaired children are assigned to regular classrooms they frequently become isolated. Isolation can occur because the child with a hearing loss has funny speech, wears a hearing aid, or utilizes some behavioral attention-getting device. This exhibited behavior could be due, in part, to the hearing loss. For example, the hearing-impaired child may attempt to monopolize a conversation because of the fear of misunderstanding conversations initiated by others. Strange and staring behavior may be nothing more than a valiant effort to speechread. And a loud or soft voice may be a function of the hearing loss, not the child's mood or personality.

It is important that the clinician help classmates and teachers understand why these behaviors occur and how they may be dissipated.

### Educational Level

Formal and informal educational tests should be used to evaluate the student's progress and to plan realistic programs for him. It is important that hearing-impaired students who are in regular classrooms be evaluated with the same instruments used to evaluate the normally hearing peer group. While there are tests which are based on norms derived from a hearing loss population, the hearing handicapped child in a regular school program is competing with normally hearing children and his progress or lack of progress should be monitored accordingly.

Speechreading and auditory training activities should be presented at a level which is commensurate to the child's level of academic functioning. Thus, it is necessary to determine the language and educational level at which he is functioning.

The evaluative procedures that can be used in determining ability or potential ability are standardized tests and informal measures of language functioning such as written and oral responses to a specified set of material.

Auditory training and speechreading material is more appropriate and meaningful to the child when presented at a language level which he comprehends.

### Family Support

The handicapped child whose problem is accepted by his family and whose family can give him educational assistance at home has increased chances for success in a regular school program. It is difficult to objectively evaluate how much educational support a parent can give his child.

Through informal interviews and regularly scheduled parent-clinician conferences, the clinician can gain some insight into how much extra help a parent can reasonably give, in addition to the education all parents provide for their children. This information is not only helpful to the clinician, but also to the student's regular classroom teacher.

For example, how realistically do parents handle extra assignments and homework? If the spelling list for the week comes home on Monday afternoon, do parents try to teach the whole list on Monday night, or do they try to distribute the work load through the week? Have the parents learned the rules for making speechreading an easier task? Do they try to make him achieve auditory discriminations which are not possible because of the limitations imposed by his hearing loss? Are the parents applying too much pressure for better communication skills from the child or do they try to hold the student to standards which are reasonable at the time? Is the parents' language output appropriate to provide a good language model for the child?

There are no right or wrong answers to the questions posed. The clinician must evaluate responses to these questions in terms of the hearing-impaired individual's needs relative to the family environment. However, through the information gleaned from this source, a more complete picture of the child's total habilitation needs can be viewed.

## AUDITORY TRAINING

Auditory training is a process used to teach an individual with hearing loss to utilize his residual hearing. This section is intended to develop a rationale for auditory training.

In an aural habilitation program, the primary emphasis should be placed on audition, using vision as a complementary modality. This philosophy dictates that early training is focused on teaching the child to use his residual hearing.

Auditory training should be organized around a specific set of objectives which are stated in behavioral terms. This type of approach will accomplish at least two goals: (1) provide a structure for lessons, and (2) provide a structure for evaluating the effectiveness of the lesson. For example, *the child will be able to discriminate auditorially between two durational cues at eighty percent efficiency across five blocks of trials. His response will be a psychomotor response.* (See Chapter VII for a more complete description of behavioral objectives.)

A careful recording of performances will furnish an on-going record of what auditory discriminations occur and when the child reaches his auditory potential.

### Factors to Consider in Training

To implement and maintain the best possible situation for listening, the training process should be *individualized* and *consistent* over time, with *appropriate* stimulus materials.

Listening training for the hearing-impaired child, in many instances, is not a group process. It is more economical in time and more beneficial for the child if the clinician provides instructional periods which are individualized. For example, the child who already has learned to make simple auditory discriminations would not be appropriately stimulated if he were placed with a child just beginning such a program. Consequently, time would be lost for both children.

Consistency refers to a planned program of listening training rather than to the fact that a child consistently wears an amplifying device all of his waking hours. The hearing aid is of little value if the user has not been taught to first maximally utilize the auditory channel.

Children who were born with a hearing loss must learn to attach meaning to sound. The process is probably not different from that which the normal hearing infant experiences. He learns to attach meaning to sound in his environment which provided food, comfort, and security. He further learns that these sounds have a variety of meanings and that he can use them to manipulate his own environment.

Children who acquire a hearing loss after the onset of language must be supplied with the experiences which help them process amplified auditory signals. Learning to listen is an ongoing process, and as the child matures, he must have structured support in refining these skills.

### Role of Amplification

The initial stages of auditory training should be devoted to getting the hearing aid on a child and then teaching him the proper care and use of the aid. In the case of the upper elementary-aged child, he should be taught the assets and limitations of his aid.

It is also an important part of a child's auditory training to explain to the classroom teacher the limitations of the hearing aid. The regular teacher also should know that amplification adds additional distortion to the listening situation of the hearing aid user. The aid amplifies all of the classroom noise, including the primary sound source (the teacher's voice). Falling books, falling pencils, restless feet, and normal movement by twenty-five or so children, provide extraneous noise, that when amplified, the hearing aid user may miss much of the pertinent message of the teacher.

The clinician should provide the teacher with basic information about how the hearing aid works, simple care of the aid, and how to insert the earmold and battery. The teacher must not be expected to take care of the child's aid; however, in an emergency situation, this knowledge would be helpful.

Most teachers, and parents for that matter, believe that once the aid is put on the child, he can hear and understand as well as his normal hearing classmates and that all of his language, speech, and educational problems will *automatically* disappear. They do not realize that the student must still learn to resolve these problems and that amplification may only be an *aid not a solution.* This point cannot be emphasized enough.

Obviously, these aforementioned facts should be presented to both teacher and parents when the aid is first considered for the student. This information may help discourage unrealistic expectations from amplification. Still, the clinician may find that after his efforts to educate parents and teachers, some will still wonder why the student doesn't perform like his normal hearing classmates when he wears his aid.

Not all hearing-impaired children will benefit from a hearing aid. Some children whose pure-tone audiograms exhibit relatively normal responses to the lower frequencies are usually poor candidates for aids. The local audiologist should be available to reiterate to the teacher and the clinician why this type of hearing loss does not respond well to amplification.

### Appropriate Seating

Appropriate seating must be provided for the hearing-impaired student in the classroom. This seat is not necessarily the front row, and the placement will vary with the child and his problem. Permit the youngster to move the appropriate distance, closer to or farther from the source of activities, thereby making communication easier. For example, the child with a hearing aid does not necessarily want to be near the record player speaker or next to the piano sounding board because it may be too loud; yet he may wish to be close to the teacher when she is explaining something.

### Approaches to Auditory Training

Suggestions for auditory training are many and varied. Since there is already a large amount of suggested lesson material in print from a variety of sources (one good example is by Lowell and Stoner, 1960), the ideas contained here will be centered around the child, his classroom, and his daily activities.

School-age children should have therapy from appropriate sources of material. One of the richest sources is from the children's own classroom material. Word lists from all subject matter areas (reading, arithmetic, spelling, science, social studies), become the lesson materials for auditory training, speechreading and other communication skills.

The lower, primary-age child is generally concerned with himself, his home and his school. As he matures, his interests become broader; therefore, the range of available material becomes greater.

The rule of thumb in preparing materials is that the more relevant the material and the more a child is involved in the situation (active therapy as opposed to passive therapy), the more likely he will improve his communication skills.

The following are suggested methods and materials for use in auditory training programs for the hearing-impaired child in the regular classroom:

1. Record new vocabulary from reading, spelling, math etc., on tape loops or other play-back devices so that the hearing-impaired student can have his own material for independent practice.
2. Historical and geographical facts which most children learn can be programmed for auditory training. For example, a President of the United States could be the stimulus and the response could be some well-known facts about him. The name of a state could be given and the response would be the capital. This source has endless possibilities. To develop better response skills for *what* and *huh*, teach for auditory recognition such phrases as *What did you say?*, *Please repeat that last sentence?*, *Come again?*, *Do you spell that with an /e/ or an /i/?*, and other colloquial possibilities.
3. Important terminology from the various sports events can be taught as an auditory discrimination task. In addition to the

terminology, names of local and professional athletes can be taught.

4. Start compiling a list of vocabulary and phrases which are common to school social functions. These words and phrases are especially important to the high school youngster. Colloquial language of the peer group can be organized into an auditory discrimination lesson. Such phrases as *groovy, far-out, bug off, ditch, give me some slack,* are not very appealing terms to adults; however, this is the language of many teenagers, and it is functional language for them.

5. Situational language makes interesting lesson material. For example, the language used when you first enter a restaurant is predictable. *Do you have a reservation? How many please? May I take your order? Would you like baked potato or french fries? What kind of dressing would you like on your salad?* An examination of this material reveals that auditory discriminations may be made on the basis of several parameters such as duration, phonetic differences, and others.

6. It is important socially for the hearing-impaired student to know the names of his classmates. Auditory recognition of classmates' names can be a useful, fun-type activity.

7. All children are interested in popular music. Since the beginning of recorded music there has been a generation gap between child and adult interests. In spite of adult reaction to popular music, this is a rich source of material for aural habilitation for all school age children. Music can provide the student with listening training for rate, rhythm, intonation patterns and new vocabulary in addition to keeping him socially current with his peer group. Familiarize the student with music appropriate for his age level. Nursery rhymes are appropriate for the very young, and pop music can be used with the high school student. Words can be transcribed so the child can follow the record as it plays.

### Summary

To summarize and re-emphasize the importance of developing good listening skills from auditory training, the following points are important for the clinician to remember: (1) The hearing-impaired student must be fitted with an amplifying device, if appropriate; (2) audition is the primarily trained sense with vision being trained as the complementary sense; (3) listening training is an individual process as opposed to a group process; (4) listening training must be well planned and consistently administered; (5) lesson planning is based on the (a) amount of hearing loss, (b) the audiometric configuration, (c) the level of linguistic functioning, and (d) meaningful material selected from the child's environment; and (6) parents, teachers, and other adults in the child's environment must be aware of the nature, extent, and limitations of his hearing problem.

## SPEECHREADING

Speechreading (lipreading) is the term most frequently used when referring to the procedure which hearing-impaired individuals use to visually process information. Perhaps visual communication is a better term. It implies that the individual takes in information from the lips, facial expressions and bodily gestures to improve his understanding of spoken language. In other words, body language, in addition to spoken language, provides cues for verbal and non-verbal communication.

Visual communication, as it applies to the hearing-impaired child, can be assumed to be a process which the individual uses to fill in information which cannot be taken in auditorially. The individual whose hearing loss imposes limitations in fully understanding conversational speech will become more effective when he can substitute visual cues for missing auditory ones.

Many children acquire speechreading skills by merely observing speakers. They are not consciously aware of the process. They do become aware of the fact that careful observation of a speaker's face assists them in the communication process. Other children must be systematically taught speechreading skills.

### Testing Speechreading Ability

Tests to evaluate speechreading skills are not as numerous or commonly known as the techniques for evaluating auditory functioning. For children up to eight or nine years of age, a test described by Butts and Chreist (1968) can be used. Even though it was not necessarily designed for children, the Utley Test of Lipreading Ability (1946) may be a useful evaluation procedure.

In addition to formal tests, it is recommended that clinician-made tests be devised utilizing the functional language used by the hearing-impaired child's peer group.

A final but most important area of testing which should be acquired are tests of visual discrimination. Every hearing-impaired child should have regular, thorough examination of his eyes by the appropriate medical specialist.

### Acquisition of Basic Skills

Once a base-rate for speechreading ability has been determined, appropriate teaching should begin. Some of the basic skills the speechreader should acquire are as follows:

1. The speechreading process should be synthetic as opposed to elemental. It is more important to grasp ideas rather than bits and pieces of a conversation. The student who attempts to see every spoken word finds himself hopelessly lost as far as the ongoing conversation is concerned.
2. Information can be acquired by closely observing the speaker. A child in a regular classroom must learn to attend to the teacher both auditorially and visually as she moves about the room. A teacher is not a stationary object.
3. People differ on many dimensions. Lips are different shapes and sizes; rate of speech differs from person to person; precision in articulation varies with individuals, and lipstick, pencils, cigarettes, cigars, pipes, mustaches, and other miscellaneous items are hazards for speechreading. The student must learn early that some people will attempt to make communication easier, and others, for a variety of reasons, are unable to do so.
4. Hearing-impaired children at the intermediate grade levels and above, should be taught that features of conventional speech have likenesses and differences. At earlier age levels, children have been taught to discriminate between homophoneous words and sounds primarily from contextural clues.

*Suggestions for Speechreading Activities*

Suggested activities are not to be construed as lesson plans. The material presented here is to be used as a guide to stimulate the clinician's thinking about sources of functional materials which are appropriate and readily available.

1. Many of the suggestions used for auditory training may also be used as visual stimuli. For example, the vocabulary from reading, math, and science can be used as speechreading exercises.
2. When hearing-impaired children have difficulty speechreading a conversation, repeating the statement using the same words will not always make them understand. Restating the same idea using different words will help them understand better.
3. Encourage the child to participate in classroom activities, both curricular and extra-curricular, which will give him a variety of people and situations for speechreading practice.
4. Encourage his peer group, teachers, and parents to use a normal rate of speech. Exaggerated articulation makes speechreading more difficult.
5. At the appropriate time (this will vary with individual children), special lessons dealing with the identification of the elements of speech should be taught. For example, he should become aware of common and different features of /p/, /b/, and /m/. In all probability, the speechreader is already aware that there are visual likenesses and differences in speech, so this activity will merely provide him with the reasons why these variables exist.

In addition to the everyday instructional items, there are many printed sources of general material which can be individualized. Many of these sources categorize materials according to age and interest levels. One of these very fine sources is Jeffers and Barley (1971, Chapter VI).

## SUMMARY

Hearing-impaired children in the regular school program do not always receive the most appropriate habilitation services. In order to provide the best possible service, a careful speechreading, auditory and language evaluation must be performed. From this evaluation, the child's habilitation program is carefully structured.

The child's habilitation program must first focus on training him to use his residual hearing to its maximum potential. This approach then dictates that speechreading becomes a complementary modality for learning new speech and language. Only through careful programming of auditory training and speechreading will this task be accomplished.

## REFERENCES

Butts, D. S., and Chreist, F. M.: A speechreading test for young children. *Volta Rev, 70:*225-244, 1968.

Jeffers, J., and Barley, M.: *Speechreading.* Springfield, Thomas, 1971.

Lowell, E., and Stoner, M.: *Play it by ear. Auditory Training Games.* Wolfer, 1960.

Utley, J.: A test of lip reading ability. *J Speech Hearing Dis, 11:*109-116, 1946.

# CHAPTER IX

# HEARING AIDS: THEIR APPLICATIONS AND LIMITATIONS FOR THE HEARING-IMPAIRED CHILD

## WILLIAM R. HODGSON

THE COMPLETELY DEAF person responds to no sound. The nature of his problem may be obvious. But the hearing-impaired child has an invisible handicap. He can hear some sounds but not others, and as a result, he may respond inconsistently or inappropriately. His behavior may suggest inattention, mental retardation or even an emotional disorder.

A hearing aid informs others of the nature of the child's disorder. It may also help to alleviate the problem or, if improperly used, create new ones. It is the intent of this chapter to help the clinician meet the amplification needs of the hearing-impaired child. Hearing aids are described, and their care and use are discussed.

## PURPOSE OF A HEARING AID

Electronic hearing aids have been described as miniature public address systems. That is, although small enough to be worn, they have essentially the same components and perform the same function as a public address system. The purpose of a hearing aid is to make sound louder for a hearing-impaired listener.

## ADVANTAGES AND LIMITATIONS OF A HEARING AID

Amplification does not correct hearing problems with the efficiency that glasses correct many types of defective vision. The best hearing aid does not return the ear to normal function nor, of course, does it automatically compensate for the accumulated deficit of language, speech, and auditory responsivity that accompanies a hearing loss of long standing.

161

Many factors influence hearing aid use. From an auditory viewpoint, successful hearing aid use focuses on two aspects of the ear's performance, auditory sensitivity and auditory discrimination ability. Sensitivity refers to how intense sound has to be before a person can hear it, and discrimination ability relates to how clearly a person can experience sound, once it is loud enough for him to hear.

Hearing aids are available with sufficient power to make sounds audible to even the severely hard of hearing. However, as a generalization, *hearing aids make sounds louder but not any clearer.* Herein lies the principal limitation of the hearing aid. Once the amplifying power of the aid makes speech audible, intelligibility of speech will be mostly dependent on the discrimination ability of the impaired ear. Stated differently, the hearing aid cannot remove the distortion generated in the defective ear. Because of this fact, the remaining discrimination ability of the impaired ear is a critical factor in the success of hearing aid use.

The better the discrimination ability, the greater the probability of a satisfied hearing aid wearer. Individuals with conductive-type hearing loss (a blockage of sound energy as it passes through the outer or middle ear) ordinarily retain normal discrimination ability. Once amplification compensates for their loss of sensitivity, they understand speech well. Therefore, they can be very good hearing aid candidates. However, most conductive losses are potentially correctable by medicine or surgery, so relatively few people with conductive loss prefer hearing aids.

If the hearing loss comes from a deficit in the inner ear (called a nerve or sensorineural loss) both sensitivity and discrimination ability will be impaired. In a general sense, the hearing aid can alleviate only the problem associated with sensitivity. Nevertheless, the great majority of people wearing hearing aids have sensorineural loss. Many people with such loss retain good enough discrimination ability to understand amplified speech. Others are satisfied to wear aids that give them only partial understanding, help them with lipreading, or at least keep them in contact with their auditory environment. Thus, most people with sensorineural loss can get some help from a hearing aid, provided they learn to use it properly.

The advantages and limitations of a hearing aid can be stated simply. Hearing aids are available with enough amplifying power to make speech audible to almost anyone, but the intelligibility of this amplified speech is attendant on the fidelity of the impaired ear.

## PHYSICAL CHARACTERISTICS OF A HEARING AID

### Basic Components

All hearing aids, regardless of type, have certain components, as shown in Figure 9-1. The *microphone*, located behind a grill or small opening in the case, changes sound energy into an electrical signal. The *amplifier* increases the magnitude of the electrical signal, drawing its power from the *battery*. The hearing aid earphone, or *receiver* changes the amplified electrical signal back into sound energy for the hearing aid user.

### Types of Hearing Aids

Wearable hearing aids are of two types, *body-worn* and *at-the-ear*. A body-worn aid is shown in Figure 9-2. The case (which houses the microphone, amplifier, and battery) is carried in a pocket or other enclosure located on the body of the user. The

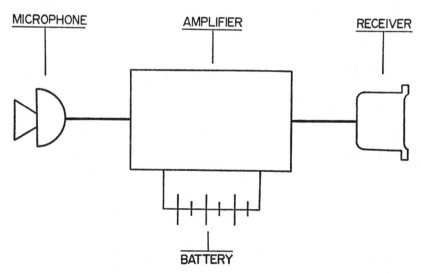

Figure 9-1. Block diagram of the basic components of a hearing aid.

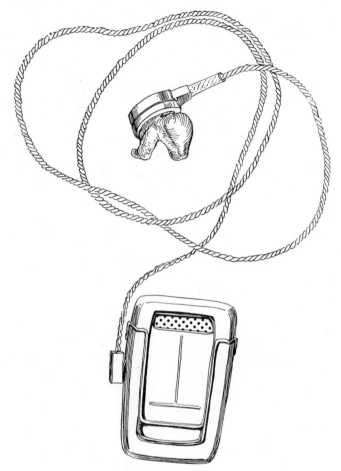

Figure 9-2. A body-worn hearing aid.

receiver is held in the aided ear by the earmold. A connecting cord carries the electrical signal from the hearing aid amplifier to the receiver.

Many body aids have top-mounted microphones, i.e. the microphone is located on the top of the case rather than on the front. Such top-mounted microphones reduce noise encountered with a front-mounted microphone when clothing movements occur against the microphone grill. Especially in children, however, top-mounted microphones are exposed and vulnerable to spilled food and other debris which may impair their function.

At-the-ear aids are usually classified as *behind-the-ear, eyeglass,* or *in-the-ear*. Examples of each type are shown in Figure 9-3. While the components of the ear-level aids are similar to the body-worn aids, they are smaller, and the receiver is located inside the case of the aid with sound traveling from the aid's receiver through a tube, into the earmold and on into the ear.

Body-worn aids are traditionally more powerful than at-the-ear aids and are therefore appropriate for the most severely

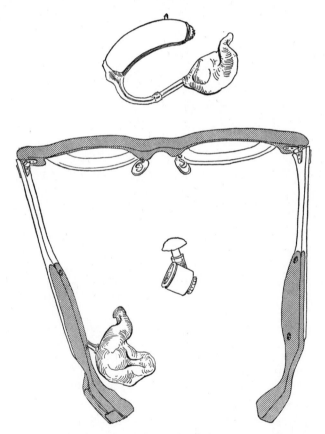

Figure 9-3. At-the-ear hearing aids. Behind-the-ear, eye-glass, and in-the-ear types are shown.

hard-of-hearing. Other things being equal, an at-the-ear aid is preferable if the magnitude of loss is within its amplifying range, since such an aid permits ear-level hearing (effectively the wearer's ear is where the hearing aid microphone is located) and is preferable cosmetically.

## Earmolds

The standard hearing aid earmold has as its purpose securely coupling the hearing aid receiver to the ear. The earmold must fit the ear well and do its job without substantial acoustic leaks. If enough sound leaks out and re-enters the hearing aid microphone, a feedback loop results, generating a high-pitch whistle or squeal. The greater the gain of the aid, the better the mold must fit to prevent this feedback. Other sources of sound leakage are where the receiver snaps on to the earmold (body aids) or where the sound tube connects to the earmold of the hearing aid (at-the-ear aids). If feedback is a problem, wearing the case of the body aid as far as possible from the ear containing the earmold and receiver may resolve the problem.

Some earmolds, called *vented* or *open* earmolds, are used to modify the frequency response of the hearing aid. Since these molds have openings designed to let some sound leak out, they cannot be used with very high gain instruments since this would result in feedback problems.

## Hearing Aid Controls

Hearing aids ordinarily have one or more external controls which permit adjustment of the operating characteristics of the aid. The *volume (or gain) control* is similar to that of a radio. It permits the wearer to adjust the amount that the aid will intensify incoming signals. An *off-on switch* may be incorporated into the volume control, although at-the-ear aids are often turned off by pulling the battery compartment slightly away from its normal position.

The volume control of a body-worn aid is often marked in numbers (such as zero to ten) to indicate the amount of amplification. However, these gain controls are usually not linear. It should not be assumed that a gain control setting of five represents half the amplification of an aid, if ten is the top number on the control. In all likelihood the aid will deliver *more* than half of its available amplification when the gain control is turned half open, i.e. to five in the previously cited example. Sample taper characteristics (gain control setting versus the actual increase in amplification) are shown in Figure 9-4 to illustrate the fact that the gain of the hearing aid is not linear with regard to its numerical dial settings.

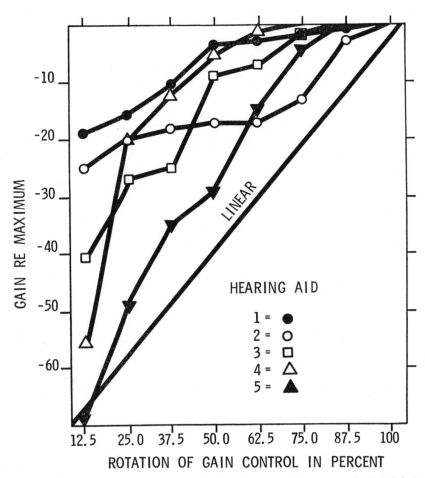

Figure 9-4. Sample taper characteristics of various hearing aids. Modified from Kasten, R., and Lotterman, S.: Influence of hearing aid gain control rotation on acoustic gain. *J Auditory Res*, 9:35-39, 1969.

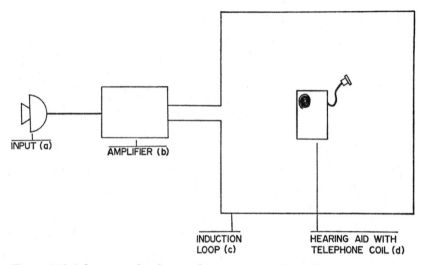

INPUT (a)   AMPLIFIER (b)

INDUCTION
LOOP (c)

HEARING AID WITH
TELEPHONE COIL (d)

Figure 9-5. Schematic of induction loop system used in classroom amplification. The teacher's voice is (a) picked up by a microphone and (b) amplified. The amplified signal passing through the induction loop (c) creates a fluctuating magnetic field. A child inside the field wearing a hearing aid (d) hears the teacher's voice when the aid's telephone coil responds to the magnetic signal.

Many body-type aids have an externally-operated *tone control* which gives some relative emphasis to high or low frequency sounds, depending on its setting. In some aids, the tone control changes the operating characteristics enough to make the aid appropriate for different kinds of hearing loss. However, in most aids, the changes obtainable through the tone control are small. Thus, the setting may be selected according to the preference of the wearer, unless a particular setting has been recommended by the audiologist.

Some hearing aids have *internal operating controls* which are set by the dealer at the time of purchase. These controls effect sizable changes in the characteristics of the aid, making it appropriate for an individual hearing loss.

Most body-type aids and some at-the-ear aids have a *telephone coil* built into their circuitry. In telephone conversations, this device can take the place of the hearing aid microphone. It is sensitive to the magnetic field generated by a telephone receiver and permits the user of the aid to receive amplified telephone conversations through his hearing aid. Since the telephone coil does not respond to room noise, a quieter signal results.

The above described principle has been applied to classroom amplification for hard-of-hearing children, as shown in Figure 9-5. It is known as an induction loop system. In such an arrangement, the transfer of the teacher's voice to the student's hearing aid is via electrical and magnetic energy from the wire loop rather than from acoustic energy traveling across the room. The result is a stronger speech signal relative to the noise in the room because the signal source (the teacher's voice) is closer to the loop system microphone than when it must travel across the room to the hearing aid microphone.

## ACOUSTIC CHARACTERISTICS OF THE HEARING AID

The electroacoustic characteristics of a hearing aid determine how it operates and whether or not it is appropriate for a person with a given hearing loss. The characteristics most frequently mentioned are (1) gain, (2) frequency response, (3) maximum power output, and (4) harmonic distortion.

### Gain

The maximum gain of an aid reflects how much it will amplify sound with the gain control fully on. Simply stated, gain (reported in decibels) is output minus input. As the volume control is turned up, gain increases. Hearing aids are available with maximum gain from about twenty-five dB to more than seventy-five dB. Obviously, the more severe the loss the greater should be the maximum gain of the aid.

### Frequency Response

Frequency response describes the frequency range which an aid will transmit and amplify as well as the amount of amplification given to each frequency within the aid's operating range. Figure 9-6 shows the frequency response of a typical hearing aid. One can see that the aid amplifies some frequencies more than others, i.e. the frequency response is uneven.

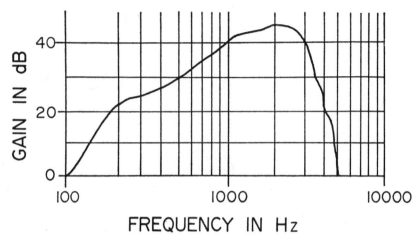

FREQUENCY IN Hz

Figure 9-6. Frequency response of a representative hearing aid. The frequency range of this aid is from three hundred sixty to forty-one hundred Hz.

Sometimes an uneven frequency response is purposeful. For example, aids with high frequency emphasis (greater amplification of high frequencies) are used by people who have high frequency loss. In other instances, the uneven frequency response represents the compromises that result when the aid's components are miniaturized enough to fit into a case that tucks in a pocket or behind the ear. The typical frequency range (lower and upper limit of useful amplification) is about three hundred to four thousand Hz.

### Maximum Power Output

All hearing aids have a maximum power output. The output limiter on a hearing aid is like the governor on an automobile. If a car has a governor, after a specified speed is reached, it will go no faster no matter how much the accelerator is depressed. The governor is a safety device which limits the car's speed. The hearing aid's output limiter is a safety device which limits its output. The output will not go beyond a specified level no matter how much the input or the gain is increased. This limitation insures that the aid's output will not be painful or harmful to the wearer's ear. Thus, it helps him tolerate intense sounds that come through the aid.

### Harmonic Distortion

Unfortunately, the more the aid's limiter represses the output, the more the amplifier is overdriven. Overdriving the amplifier results in harmonic distortion to which the wearer must listen. A good deal of harmonic distortion can occur without reducing intelligibility of speech, although the quality of speech becomes less desirable. Eventually, however, as harmonic distortion increases, the speech signal is changed enough that it becomes less intelligible.

Some hearing aids achieve output limitation in a fashion that results in less harmonic distortion when intense sounds are encountered. These are aids with automatic gain control. Although this automatic circuit sometimes introduces its own problems to hearing aid use, it is a helpful device for those who have a low tolerance threshold for loud sounds and must wear aids with a low maximum power output.

### TAKING CARE OF A HEARING AID

Hearing aid care is considered at this point, rather than later, to acquaint the reader with the hearing aid and its parts before the evaluation and selection of a hearing aid are considered.

### Wearing the Aid

Provisions should be made for a body aid to be worn securely especially when it is used by a young child. Figure 9-7 shows the type of carrier garment that is commonly used. Ideally, this garment is worn outside the clothing, primarily to make the controls of the aid available for adjusting, but also to reduce the layers of interfering clothing covering the aid's microphone.

The aid must fit snugly into the cloth pocket of the carrier garment so that contact noise is not generated as the aid shifts around in response to body movement. It is also important that the pocket of the garment be designed so the controls of the aid are accessible. These problems are reduced with an at-the-ear aid.

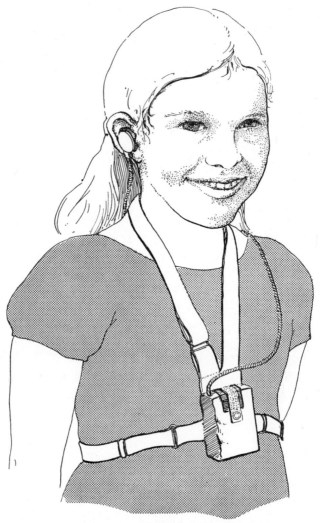

Figure 9-7. Carrier garment for a body-worn hearing aid.

However, keeping such an aid on the head depends on a well-fitting earmold and secure attachment of the aid to the earmold via its sound conducting tubing.

### Cords

The cord of a body-worn aid (the electrical connection between aid and receiver) is vulnerable. Normal wear may break the wiring inside the cord although the outer insulation remains intact. This invisible disruption of the electrical signal often results in intermittent performance of the hearing aid. It is a good idea to keep on hand a spare cord of the proper length.

### Earmolds

The earmold should be kept clean. The sound channel which passes through the earmold should be kept clear of earwax which can block the channel and impede sound. If the earmold is detachable it may be washed in soapy water.

Damaged or broken earmolds should be replaced immediately, for they may cause injury to the wearer. Likewise, earmolds which have been outgrown and are too small for the child should be replaced. If the mold does not fit properly, it will not only have a tendency to fall out of the ear but feedback (squealing) will be a problem.

### Battery

Attention to the battery is important. The battery which is correct for the individual aid must be used. Some aids operate on either a mercury or a silver-oxide battery (the latter supplying a little more gain), so the recommendation for the proper battery should be known and followed.

The battery must be inserted properly, with the *plus-marked* end of the battery matched to the *plus mark* in the hearing aid's battery compartment. The battery should fit snugly into its compartment. If it fits loosely against the contacts, intermittent response from the aid may result.

If the aid is to be unused for any period of time, longer than overnight, the battery should be removed from the aid. A dead battery can leak and damage the aid.

Most important for good battery use is the determination of when a battery should be discarded, for a battery does not retain perfect efficiency to the end of its life. A battery tester (voltmeter) is helpful in this respect. If the measured voltage is less than that specified (1.4 volts for a mercury battery and 1.5 volts for silver-oxide), the battery should be discarded. Batteries should be tested daily at the end of their operating day. Unused overnight, a weak battery may revitalize long enough, following its overnight rest, to pass an early morning battery check, only to fail shortly afterward.

### Listening Check

The most critical aspect of hearing aid care is a daily listening check to be sure the aid is functioning properly. *There is no way to be sure that a hearing aid is working right except to listen to it.* Since young children may not be able to detect and report hearing aid malfunction, it is important that someone, a parent or a teacher, listen to the aid daily. Especially with behind-the-ear aids, a listening device such as the hearing aid stethoscope, shown in Figure 9-8, is needed for the listening check.

While listening to the hearing aid, check the following things. Turn the gain control up and down slowly. Listen for noise generated by the turning of the control. Increase the gain control to a level that is appropriately loud for the power of the aid. Listen for an accompanying relatively smooth increase in loudness. Defective aids may continue to operate with an increase in the gain control but with a loss of power. Listen, too, for the same clarity of speech that the aid customarily produces. Loss of either loudness or clarity may be caused by a weak battery. If there are problems put in a new battery and listen again.

Next, if you are listening to a body-type aid, roll the cord between your fingers, holding the cord first where it attaches to the receiver and then where it attaches to the aid (these are the two areas of greatest stress and where cords are most likely to break). If the cord is defective, a noisy or intermittent signal will result. The cord should be replaced. Check the terminals where the cord plugs into the aid and the receiver. If these connections are loose, they need repair.

Finally, tap the hearing aid case gently to see if there are loose components which generate noise when jarred. Having performed these simple operations you can be sure, from listening to the aid, that it is working well. If the aid is defective, it should be returned to the dealer for repairs.

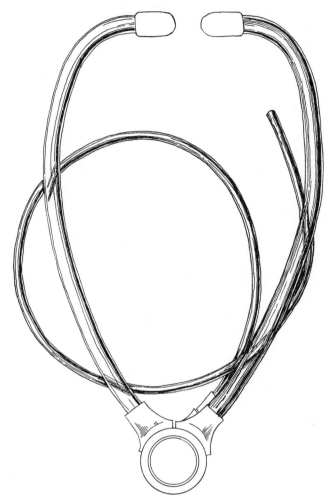

Figure 9-8. Hearing aid stethoscope. Available from Hal-Hen Company, 36-14, 11th St., Long Island City, New Jersey 11106.

## Protecting the Aid

At the risk of reviewing the obvious, each of the following is potentially harmful to a hearing aid and should be avoided to protect the aid: (a) falls or blows of any kind; (b) liquid or moisture; (c) sand, dirt, or any other foreign substance (the microphone via its covering grill or opening being particularly susceptible); (d) extremes of temperature; (e) hair sprays and medicinal sprays; and (f) teeth of dogs or children when applied forcibly to the case of the hearing aid.

## SELECTING A HEARING AID

Need and benefit are the two concerns that determine the usefulness of a hearing aid to a hearing-impaired person. Need for a hearing aid can usually be determined by the magnitude of hearing loss. Benefit to be gained from hearing aid use is closely associated with auditory discrimination ability.

To explain, as an individual's hearing loss grows greater, his need for amplification increases. He has more need for a hearing aid to make sounds more intense so that he can hear them at a comfortable and useful level. However, it is his auditory discrimination ability, his ability to differentiate between sounds, which determines how well he can benefit from the amplification. A person who has a large loss of hearing sensitivity and retains good auditory discrimination ability is a good hearing aid candidate. An individual with a similar loss of sensitivity but poorer discrimination is less likely to be satisfied with his hearing aid. The fact that it makes sounds audible he otherwise could not hear may induce him to wear it. He will complain, however, that speech is not clear, and he will still have some difficulty understanding.

In general, an ideal *aided* speech threshold (i.e. level at which the person can just hear and repeat about fifty percent of the words presented to him) is about twenty decibels poorer than the speech threshold of normal hearing persons. Such amplification depends on the gain of the hearing aid.

Mild hearing losses are best served by aids with mild maximum gain. More severe losses require aids with greater gain. Aids with very high maximum gain are available today, sufficient to make speech *audible* for even the most severe hearing losses. Remember, however, that the intelligibility of such aided speech is primarily a function of the listener's ear (as well as his level of receptive language, of course) although the fidelity of the hearing aid is also a factor.

While the gain of an aid must be great enough to insure audibility, the *maximum power output* of the aid must be tolerable to the user. That is, when already loud sounds are additionally amplified by the aid, the resulting output must be tolerable. If it is not, an aid with a lower maximum power output must be selected.

It is the responsibility of the audiologist to determine need and benefit regarding hearing aid use. It is also his task to recommend to the hearing aid dealer the approximate operating characteristics of the hearing aid. These include maximum gain, maximum power output, and frequency response characteristics.

### SEVERAL POTENTIAL HEARING AID USERS

The following examples relate audibility, tolerability, and intelligibility to hearing aid use. Figure 9-9 shows the audiogram

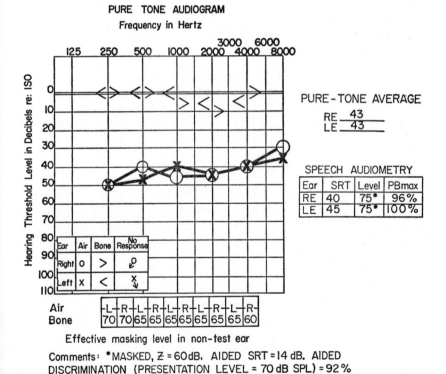

Comments: *MASKED, $\bar{Z}$ = 60dB. AIDED SRT = 14 dB. AIDED DISCRIMINATION (PRESENTATION LEVEL = 70 dB SPL) = 92%

Figure 9-9. Conductive hearing loss. A mild gain aid gives good audibility, and normal discrimination ability is retained.

of a child with a fluctuating conductive hearing loss. This child has normal hearing much of the time but has a periodic conductive loss which often approximates the magnitude shown. Therefore, he is a part-time hearing aid wearer, using his hearing aid on days when his hearing is reduced. He wears a behind-the-ear aid on his right ear. It is a mild gain aid which makes conversational voice comfortably loud, and the child, when listening to conversational level speech, obtained a discrimination score of ninety-two percent. Because he has no tolerance problems for loud sounds and retains excellent auditory discrimination ability, he is a very good hearing aid candidate.

Most people who wear hearing aids have sensorineural loss, rather than conductive loss. Figure 9-10 shows the audiogram of a four-year-old with a moderate sensorineural loss. This boy was fitted with a medium-gain aid on his right ear. Because of his

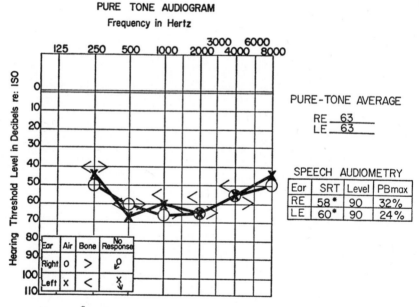

Comments: *SELECTED SPONDEES. RELIABILITY GOOD. BODY-TYPE AID ON RIGHT EAR (GAIN 5, TONE M): AIDED SRT = 16 dB.

Figure 9-10. Moderate sensorineural loss. A body-worn aid was used with good results.

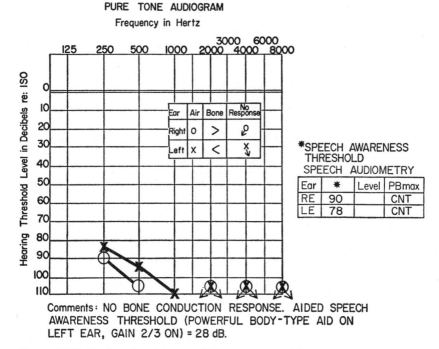

Figure 9-11. Profound sensorineural loss. A powerful body-worn aid makes speech audible but not intelligible.

young age, a body-type aid was used although perhaps an at-the-ear aid would have been as suitable (and, from an auditory standpoint, better). A good aided-speech threshold (sixteen dB) was obtained while discrimination scores were poor. *The child's language retardation (due to the congenital hearing loss) accounts for a substantial part of the reduction in the discrimination scores.* In other words, his actual discrimination ability, while certainly not perfect, is better than the scores suggest. The aid made speech quite audible for the child, and his ability to discriminate speech sounds was good enough to make him a happy hearing aid user.

The audiogram in Figure 9-11 is that of a child with a profound sensorineural loss and no responses above one thousand Hz. A powerful body-type aid (this loss is beyond the effective range of at-the-ear aids) makes speech audible. However, because the child's hearing is limited to the low frequencies, the ability to understand speech by listening to it cannot be expected to develop. With training, the child's hearing should become a useful source of information which will nevertheless remain secondary in importance to visual input.

## LEARNING TO USE A HEARING AID

A person's first experiences with hearing aid use are crucial to (1) whether or not he will accept the hearing aid and (2) how efficiently he learns to use it. Without adequate preparation, the new hearing aid wearer may simply be overwhelmed with a cacophony of unexpected sound, from which he cannot extract a desired signal, and which may cause him to reject the aid. Or a child with an extreme loss, not having learned to respond to sound consistently, without the proper training may simply learn to wear the aid like another article of clothing, perhaps not bothering to keep the aid turned on or to report when batteries need replacing.

The person with a hearing loss needs counseling to help him understand his hearing loss. In the case of a child, this applies to his parents and teachers. Both parties need information regarding realistic expectations for hearing aid use. It is important that, as part of an audiological evaluation, the audiologist explain the nature and extent of the loss and how much help can be expected from a hearing aid.

### Introducing Amplification

Some psychological preparation is necessary in almost every case *before* hearing aid use is attempted. The person who will wear the aid needs help through counseling and demonstration. He needs to be prepared for the unexpected noise which will confront him when he first wears the aid. Eventually, if he wears the aid long enough, the noise that, at first, was so overwhelming should no longer be a problem. However, many people discard their aids before this adaptation occurs. For this reason, it is advisable in most cases to limit hearing aid use, at first, to brief periods of listening in a quiet place. This initial practice in a controlled acoustic environment gives the child a chance to adapt to the noise of amplification gradually and at the same time helps him become accustomed to the different quality of speech and other sounds which come through the hearing aid. Gradually exposure can be extended and sounds of greater complexity and intensity introduced, with an attempt made to discontinue each practice session before the child tires or objects.

### Cosmetic Factors

Cosmetic concerns are bound to arise, especially in older children. Sometimes the concern of a teenager about appearing different than his peers through the use of the hearing aid is a problem of such intensity that it is simply insoluble. Since it is a problem with an emotional base, it may do no good to point out that a behind-the-ear aid is inconspicuous to the point of invisibility, or that the child's behavior without the help of the hearing aid is likely to appear more peculiar than with it. Certainly, these facts and other logical approaches should be explored. However, if cosmetic concerns are great, they may best be reduced by the understanding and support of parents and teachers. Positive reinforcement, such as emphasis on the help a hearing aid can give rather than the problems that result without hearing aid use, may be helpful. Assistance from successful hearing aid users in the community, people who have faced the problem of adjusting to a hearing aid, may also be helpful.

### Adjusting the Hearing Aid

The hearing aid user must learn to operate the aid himself. He must learn how to put it on, take it off, and set the gain control for optimum listening.

The simple act of putting the hearing aid on (which consists of getting the earmold snugly in the ear) is surprisingly difficult at first. If the earmold is not completely seated, sound will leak out and squealing will result. The hearing aid should be turned off while it is being placed in the ear. It may help the new wearer to look in a mirror as he puts the aid on. Soon the act of putting the aid on will be easy and the procedure automatic, but the new wearer will need some assistance and encouragement.

Learning to set the gain control properly is crucial to successful hearing aid use. There are two important points to remember: (1) The gain should be adjusted to a level that produces comfortable loudness for existing sound levels, and (2) the adjustment of the gain should be *by ear,* not by eye. That is, the wearer should turn up the gain until sounds are loud enough, not by looking at the gain control and setting it at *number 6* or *half-way on.*

Properly, the wearer will need to adjust the gain of his aid to comfortable loudness for existing sound levels. This means, of course, he will have to change the gain of his aid from time to time, as the sound levels around him change. Obviously, he should not fiddle with the gain control, continuously trying to adjust to each momentary change in the intensity of surrounding sounds. Rather, he should turn the gain control up when he is in an environment which is, for the most part, quiet and turn the gain down to a comfortable listening level as the surroundings become noisier. In very noisy places (e.g. at a pep rally) most children will turn their aids off entirely.

Setting the gain control for effective listening, once learned, becomes automatic. Unless the hearing aid wearer has help in learning, he is likely to leave the gain too low for best listening, especially if he acquires the habit of leaving the gain always at one level. This level will have to be at a point which is comfortable in noisy surroundings and therefore insufficient in quieter places.

### *Environmental Noise*

A good *signal-to-noise ratio* (SNR) is important to the hearing aid wearer, especially in classroom use. SNR means the intensity of the desired signal (speech, usually) relative to interfering noise. Thus a SNR of zero dB results when speech and noise are equally loud. A *plus* SNR means the speech is more intense than interfering noise. A minus SNR means just the reverse.

People with sensorineural hearing loss perform inordinately poorly listening in noise. Specifically, in noisy places, their auditory discrimination ability drops more than listeners with normal hearing.

A good SNR can be promoted by (1) a quiet room, (2) keeping the child who wears a hearing aid as close to the speaker as possible (ideally with hearing aid microphone only a few inches from the speaker's lips), (3) talking with a strong voice, but not shouting, and (4) keeping the child as far away as possible from sources of room noise (such as open windows or doorways).

## SPECIAL CASES OF HEARING AID USE

### Monaural vs Binaural

Most people with bilateral hearing loss only wear one hearing aid. However, some wear two. Various arrangements for supplying sound to both ears are shown in Figure 9-12. Most of the

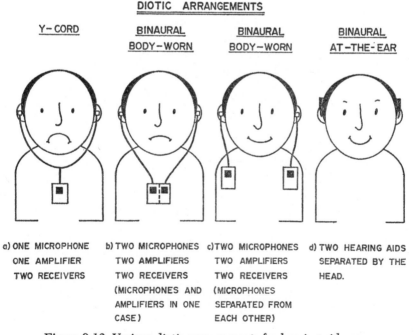

DIOTIC ARRANGEMENTS

| Y-CORD | BINAURAL BODY-WORN | BINAURAL BODY-WORN | BINAURAL AT-THE-EAR |
|---|---|---|---|
| a) ONE MICROPHONE ONE AMPLIFIER TWO RECEIVERS | b) TWO MICROPHONES TWO AMPLIFIERS TWO RECEIVERS (MICROPHONES AND AMPLIFIERS IN ONE CASE) | c) TWO MICROPHONES TWO AMPLIFIERS TWO RECEIVERS (MICROPHONES SEPARATED FROM EACH OTHER) | d) TWO HEARING AIDS SEPARATED BY THE HEAD. |

Figure 9-12. Various diotic arrangements for hearing aid use.

benefits of binaural hearing, in normal listeners, result from the fact that the ears are separated by the head (there are two spatially separated inputs to the auditory system, each carrying slightly different information).

In Figure 9-12, situation *a* (the y-cord arrangement) does not classify as binaural since the signal to both ears comes from one point, the single microphone. Situation *b* may not be a very effective binaural arrangement since the two input points (microphones) are so close together. Situation *c* while achieving microphone separation, still is not representative of normal hearing, since the ears (the microphones, or point of input into the system) remain on the chest. Only in situation *d* does the physical arrangement become reminiscent of normal hearing.

Marked superiority of binaural over monaural hearing aid use has not been substantiated. The most clearly documented advantage of binaural aids (when at-the-ear aids are worn) is elimination of the *head shadow effect*. When a person with bilateral loss wears only one aid, the effective intensity of sound is reduced as the person listens to a sound source coming from the unaided side. Stated differently, the shadow of the head, intervening between the sound source and the aided ear reduces perceived loudness of the signal (speech) substantially by the time it reaches the aided ear. This principle and the role of binaural aids in reducing it, is shown in Figure 9-13.

The head shadow reduces loudness for speech in quiet for the monaural aid wearer (Monaural in Quiet, Fig. 9-13) but the effect is intensified when the monaural wearer confronts noise emanating from a source on the side of his aided ear, while trying to listen to speech originating from the other side (Monaural in Noise, Fig. 9-13). When two at-the-ear aids are worn, speech in quiet is not influenced by the head shadow effect because it does not exist, i.e. the second aid permits speech to be received directly on either side of the head (Binaural in Quiet, Fig. 9-13). Likewise, if noise occurs on one side of the binaurally aided listener, he still has a second channel open (the other aided ear) which will receive less noise. Thus, he has a better chance to hear the speech (Binaural in Noise, Fig. 9-13).

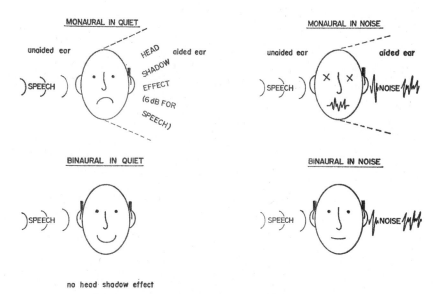

Figure 9-13. Illustration of how ear-level aids eliminate the head shadow effect and improve signal-to-noise ratio.

Binaural aids can no doubt be helpful if the listener has hearing good enough bilaterally to use at-the-ear aids and to benefit from the relatively subtle advantages which result. Most hearing aid wearers are content with the assistance (or the nuisance) supplied by one aid. Some parents supply severely or profoundly hard-of-hearing children with binaural body-type aids more in the hope than the expectation that two aids will be better than one.

### CROS-Type Aids

Various special arrangements involving crossing of the hearing aid signal from one side of the head to the other are shown in Figure 9-14. The first of these, the CROS aid, has been used with unilateral loss.

People with normal hearing on one side and no usable hearing on the other get along well in most situations. However, they cannot localize sound well and have trouble discriminating among speech sounds in noise, especially when the head shadow effect, mentioned earlier, is involved. The CROS aid, usually built into eyeglasses, gives hearing from both sides of the head, although both signals are delivered to one ear. That is, the hearing aid microphone picks up the signal on the side of the poor ear, carries it electrically to the good ear where it is changed back to sound and sent into the ear. Unaided signals from the side of the good ear enter it in the regular way. Thus, the head shadow is eliminated.

The CROS aid has been successful for the person with a unilateral loss when there have been unusual or critical demands on his hearing. For school children with unilateral loss, preferential seating close to the teacher and with the good ear directed toward the teacher, usually meets classroom needs. A hearing aid is not necessary. If, however, the child continues to have trouble in school, the possibility of an aid should be explored.

CROS aids have been more successful in helping children with bilateral, sharply falling high frequency losses than with unilateral losses. Because these aids utilize open earmolds which

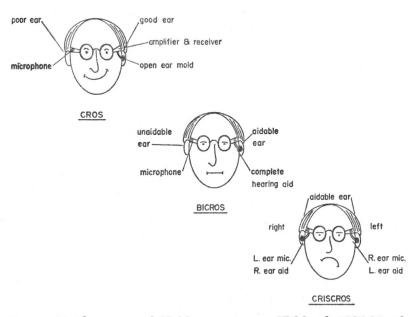

Figure 9-14. Three types of CROS arrangements: CROS aid; BICROS aid; and CRISCROS aid.

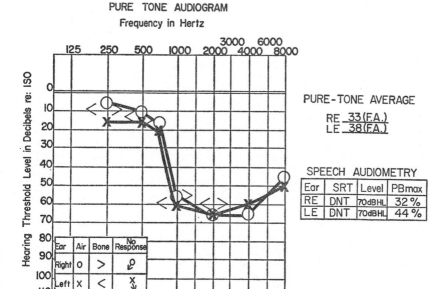

Figure 9-15. High frequency sensorineural loss appropriate for CROS aid.

do not occlude the ear canal, the child can hear the low frequencies for which he had good hearing directly without amplification and receive amplification for high frequencies where his hearing is defective. A high frequency loss appropriate for a CROS aid is in Figure 9-15.

An aid arrangement called *BICROS* (Fig. 9-14) has been used for those who have some loss, but aidable hearing on their good ear and hearing too poor to benefit from an aid on the other ear. The BICROS has a microphone on both sides of the head delivering a signal to the better ear. With BICROS an open earmold is not used.

An arrangement called CRISCROS (Fig. 9-14) has been used to reduce feedback when powerful ear-level binaural aids are used. The microphone on either side delivers a signal to the other side, thus separating each microphone from its receiver.

## SUMMARY

A hearing aid is not an end in itself but a means to an end. Properly used, it is a tool which can implement learning and communication and can facilitate language, speech, and personality development. Improperly introduced, it will be another of the many frustrating and unsuccessful experiences which lead the hearing-impaired child to give up trying to communicate and learn. It cannot be depended upon to make severely or profoundly hard-of-hearing children candidates for regular classrooms. But good hearing aid use may enable those with mild or moderate losses to get along in regular classes.

# CHAPTER X

# IMPROVING COMMUNICATION WITH THE EDUCATIONAL COMMUNITY FOR A MORE EFFECTIVE THERAPY PROGRAM

### JACK BRADSHAW

IN TRYING TO ESTABLISH an effective therapy program, the school clinician often finds himself in a rather difficult position. He may be faced with a number of problems that tend to hamper the effectiveness of his program. These obstacles often develop from a basic lack of understanding of the clinician's role in the school by other school personnel. Frequently, the clinician himself may not have a realistic view of his role in relation to other staff members and the total educational program.

Poor communication usually has its roots in two areas: (1) the clinician is an itinerant teacher who moves from school to school using methods which differ from those of the classroom teacher and (2) the clinician may not be aware of the importance of communication and cooperation with the other school personnel.

It is not difficult for the clinician who moves from school to school to lose sight of the total educational picture. He has to be here. He needs to be there. One person wants him to do this. The next person thinks he should do that. He has a hard time relating to what goes on in each building and to what happens in the various classrooms. As the frustrations build, it becomes easy to withdraw into a world of limited communication and contact with other staff members. Thus, the clinician's necessary mobility may contribute to a state of poor communication between himself and other staff members.

In many cases, poor communication may be only partially situational. Often, it may be a lack of awareness of the impor-

189

tance of understanding the viewpoints and problems of others. Therefore, the clinician working in the schools must be able to evaluate causes of a breakdown in the communication between himself and other staff members. He must be able to understand the reasons behind any misunderstandings that may arise. The clinician must also be able to contribute to and guide the improvement of communications between himself and others. Furthermore, he needs to assume the initiative and responsibility for continued good rapport.

Problems created by the clinician's unique role and the lack of understanding of his role by the teaching and administrative staff cannot be blamed entirely on either his mobility or the school staff. *It is the clinician who must take the primary responsibility for the problems which arise from a lack of understanding about his program.*

To give the clinician a more objective view of his position in the eyes of the school staff, this chapter will take a somewhat antagonistic approach. It will cast the clinician in the role of the educational interloper who is tolerated by many and accepted by few. It is hoped that through this approach, the clinician will gain insight into the need for improved communication with the educational community for a more effective therapy program.

## THE BASIS OF POOR COMMUNICATION

Poor cooperation and misunderstanding may evolve from the fact that the school administration and classroom teachers do not understand the clinician's role in the school program. Likewise, the therapist may view the administrator or teacher as having a different role, with regard to the clinician's program, than the role actually held by either the administrator or the teacher.

### Different View Points

The following sections provide an insight into the diversified view points which are often held by school administrators, classroom teachers and clinicians. A lack of awareness of these different outlooks may be at the heart of the clinician's communication problems.

THE ADMINISTRATOR: The administrator, in all probability, has never had any course work relating to speech or hearing therapy. If he is typical, he tends to think in terms of teacher-pupil ratio, curriculum, units, and schedules. He relates all of the school processes to what he knows, and all too often, all that he knows is conventional education. For instance, many school principals think the clinician can work effectively in the storage closet or boiler room because he only sees one or two children at a time. What he doesn't understand is that acoustics and space are important to an effective program.

THE CLASSROOM TEACHER: In most cases, the classroom teacher has learned to teach and think in terms of groups and classes. He finds it difficult to adjust his methodology to deal with individual differences. After all, isn't that the clinician's job to correct Johnny's speech problem? *The majority of teachers operate on the assumption that the clinician is going to cure the child's speech problem.* They don't understand that any progress that is made is the result of practice by the student in the classroom as well as when he is in therapy.

THE CLINICIAN: The clinician thinks in terms of case load, therapy procedures, and diagnostic techniques. Even though the clinician is skilled in working with communication disorders, he sometimes finds it difficult to establish communication with the school administrator. In addition, many clinicians' experiences may have been acquired exclusively in a clinical setting prior to their work in the schools. Often these clinicians see themselves and their work as being more important than that of the teacher or principal. As a result, they appear to demand that other staff members pattern their work around the therapy schedule rather than in concert with the total school program.

### The Resulting Problems

Mix all of the above ingredients together and place them within a school building and all too often the following picture emerges.

Administrator A doesn't understand therapy. Aside from providing space for the clinician, he wants nothing to do with the program. Of course, he wants a schedule. He might suggest that the clinician could work with more than one, two, or three children at one time (Teacher B can't handle them in the classroom and teach math at the same time).

Teacher C doesn't know anything about speech. Besides that, she can't take time to tell if Johnny's speech is better. She doesn't call on him often because he talks funny. She is afraid the other children might make fun of him.

Clinician D can work in the nurse's office on Tuesday or Thursday afternoon from 1:00 p.m. until 3:00 p.m. On Monday, Wednesday, and Friday mornings, he can work in a storeroom next to the gym in which physical education is being taught. Articulation problem E can't go to speech in the morning between 9:05 a.m. and 10:17 a.m. because it will interfere with his reading group, but this is the best time for the clinician to work with him.

One answer to the problem described above would be to incorporate extensive therapy training for the administrator and the teacher in their professional preparation. This would make them sensitive to the way the clinician works. Of course, then the clinician would, in turn, need extensive training in classroom teaching and administration. You can quickly see the result of this kind of education expansion, a five year B.A. or a three year M.A. program. A more reasonable answer to the dilemma comes under the heading of trying to understand the viewpoint of other staff members in an effort to establish good communications and rapport within the educational community.

### THE LACK OF INITIATION AND MAINTENANCE OF COMMUNICATION

In far too many cases, poor communication results from the lack of initiative to inform and cooperate with other staff members. Each person has assumed that others should make an effort to get along with him and realize the importance of his role in the school. As a result, there is no cooperation among the staff members. Thus, conditions remain at a static level of poor rapport or deteriorate. The resulting situation is often as follows:

the clinician begins to dislike working in the building; the teacher dislikes interrupting class to have children go to therapy; and the principal resents people disrupting the routine of his school. While the foregoing may be an exaggeration of what happens, the basic results are the same, a tense situation that works to the detriment of the students.

Consider the hypothetical case in which the clinician was starting his first year of practical experience in school work. Although he was new to the three schools he served, the therapy program was not. The previous clinician had worked on the stage in the gym of school A, in an unused closet in school B, and in a glass-enclosed office in school C. His schedule included seeing 150 students once a week in groups of five and six, for fifteen minutes.

In school A, most of the referrals seemed to be behavior problems. The teaching staff seemed to be rather cliquish and the principal had a tendency to sequester himself in his office for long periods at a time.

In school B, the principal screened all of the referrals before they were sent to the clinician. It was his rule that no one was to interrupt the teachers during the school day. The teaching staff appeared to want to cooperate but were totally afraid of the principal.

In school C, the principal also taught sixth grade. This was a small school, only one class per grade, and the teachers seemed to lack direction. As a result, they saw the clinician as someone who could help them in curriculum matters and advise them on classroom control.

The problems in these situations are ready-made. While they can't all be solved by one patented method, they all revolve around a communication problem. The point at which the clinician begins to be effective depends entirely on his ability to communicate with the staff of each school. This means that he must understand the unique problems in each school and deal with each staff with these differences in mind. In other words, the clinician can't operate in schools B or C the same as he does in school A. He has to establish himself and his program not as a separate phase of the school program but as an integrated part of it. To accomplish this, he must do the following: (1) assume the responsibility for communication; (2) exhibit a positive attitude; (3) be empathetic to the concerns of other staff members; (4) be reasonable in his demands for facilities; (5) aggressively or persistently work for a better understanding; and (6) work for better cooperation from all staff members.

## A PROPOSED SOLUTION TO COMMUNICATION PROBLEMS

It would appear that creating good rapport and communication is the result of effort on someone's part. In this case, we will assume that the responsibility for this effort rests with the clinician. This may not be fair, but the number of misunderstandings and poor working relationships that have resulted from poor communication makes fairness a moot question.

### Responsibility

The area of responsibility goes beyond an initial effort in establishing rapport. For example, the clinician cannot assume that once the building administrator has been contacted and details concerning the way the clinician will be involved in the school resolved, that everything will run smoothly. In too many cases, someone on the staff will make a comment regarding the failure of the therapist to work with this or that child or that when Johnny goes to speech the inconvenience caused by the interruption of the Bluebird's reading group is unbearable. The results of such remarks can trigger any number of problems which, in most cases, can be avoided. But the clinician must take the responsibility of maintaining an adequate level of communication and rapport with the entire staff.

If the clinician were to leave the responsibility for communications up to the principal in the previously cited school A, the clinician could not expect much understanding or cooperation from the teachers. The principal will not become any more concerned about the therapy program than he appears to be about the other educational programs. It is apparent that it is the clinician who must define his role and enlighten the staff with respect to his services. In the event that he fails to assume this responsibility, he has little right to expect his situation to differ from that of his predecessor's. Therefore, responsibility for communication is important to any change or growth of a therapy program.

## Positiveness

One of the first concepts the clinician needs to stress is that of positiveness. It is very easy to become negative in the school setting especially when other staff members have a tendency to degrade the students, the school, or other faculty members. The clinician will find, however, that if he is positive with the other staff members his problems will decrease significantly.

There are some situations and locations that are conducive to negative remarks. They include the teacher's lounge, the school lunchroom, and the office. Conversely, these places can also be ones in which positive comments will have a great effect. For example, if the clinician remarks that he sees an improvement in Susy's attention span, he helps improve the relationship between both the clinician and the teacher as well as the teacher and Susy.

A comment to the principal concerning how smoothly things operate in his building can do no harm. Instead, such positive remarks promote a more cooperative relationship between the principal and the clinician. In short, the more the clinician exhibits a positive attitude, the more he will be treated in a positive way by other staff members.

## Empathy

Empathy would, in some respects, seem to contradict the concept of positiveness. In practice, however, the clinician will find that he can be both positive and empathetic. The object of empathy is that of understanding but not necessarily agreeing with faculty members. For instance, if the teacher is deriding a student, it is enough to indicate an understanding of the teacher's problem. Agreement or argument need not become a point of the conversation.

The clinician who can be empathetic automatically has made great progress in establishing communication and rapport. As a matter of fact, he runs the risk of being placed in a therapeutic role that can cause a different kind of problem, too much empathy. In this case the clinician may find the faculty member's concern is that of a personal nature rather than objectively related to a student's problems. The clinician finds that empathy has turned to sympathy. Indeed, the teacher being sympathized with may have an emotional need that cannot be met by a specialist in the area of communication disorders.

### Reasonableness

The concept of reasonableness has been mentioned earlier, but it deserves emphasis. Everyone, including the principal, the teacher, the clinician, and the custodian (no hierarchy intended), has certain desires relating to his work and his environment. It would be nice if the needs and desires of all of these people could be fully met in a school setting but, of course, they cannot. Therefore, one needs to think in terms of what is reasonable now and what one can reasonably expect in the future.

Consider the clinician who demands a certain type of therapy room or that other staff members conform to his therapy schedule. Anticipate the cooperation he will get from the staff with whom he works, probably little. On the other hand, envision the clinician who is willing to make compromises in order to accommodate others. He is more likely to receive reasonable treatment in return.

The art of being reasonable is easy for the person who sees the overall scope of the educational program and where he fits into it. The person who is self-centered and sees his contribution to education as being the most important has a hard time understanding why others won't cooperate; why his views regarding his importance aren't shared by others; and why he never seems to be accepted as a part of the school program.

### Aggressiveness

Another point concerning rapport that seems on the surface to contradict reasonableness is that of aggressiveness. The aggressiveness referred to, however, is that of constantly trying to create better understanding by other staff of the clinician's role and the goals of his program.

If the clinician is not aggressive enough to let the principal know of his needs, in the way of facilities and cooperation, how can he expect to have them met? At the same time, if conditions are not adequate, the therapist needs to have an aggressive plan that will ultimately result in their improvement.

Again, the burden of improving or creating a desirable communicative atmosphere within a school rests with the clinician. The fulfillment of this responsiblity must be aggressively pursued. While this view point may not appear to be a fair way to perceive the area of communication, its establishment is far too important to leave to chance or to the personality characteristics of others.

## Cooperation

Good rapport and communication are important for still another reason. Most clinicians are concerned with improving their services within a school setting as well as improving the total educational program. For a clinician to effectively instigate a change, other than within his own therapy schedule, he must have the cooperation of other building personnel.

A problem often occurs when a suggestion from the clinician necessitates that the teacher or principal alter some procedure or routine. Unless these people understand the desirability of the change and are convinced to cooperate in making the change, they are liable to resist the change or at least not fully support it. On the other hand, if the staff understands how the change will help the students, they are more inclined to cooperate in accomplishing it. To go one step further, if the teacher or principal sees himself as having contributed to the idea, he becomes eager to see the change take place. Finally, if the clinician is a good salesman, the principal or teacher will think that it was his idea and will assume the responsibility for seeing that the new procedure is instituted.

## A PRACTICAL APPLICATION OF
## THE PRINCIPLES OF COMMUNICATION

In demonstrating how the above mentioned principles may work, consider the case of a fifth grade student whose auditory perception problem had caused him to fall significantly behind in reading. Although he was making progress, he was quite self-conscious about his disability, but his teacher was not flexible enough to provide individual programming. Instead, she had him in the Vultures reading group and expected the clinician to cure his auditory problem.

The clinician was quite perceptive and adept in communicating with other staff members. He suggested that the principal and the teacher meet with him to offer some suggestions about how to deal with this problem. The clinician's premise was that if the staff could offer this student reading in some setting besides the fifth grade classroom, he might be able to progress faster.

During the discussion, the teacher and principal observed that this student might be able to read some stories to the kindergarten class. This, of course, was what the clinician had in mind from the first. If he had proposed it, the chances are that the suggestion would have been met with a negative response from the teacher or principal. As a consequence of the clinician's insights, everyone wanted the plan to succeed because they had made a contribution to the solution of the problem.

It goes without saying that the clinician's insightful involvement aided the student and enhanced the chances for future cooperation with other staff members. From the communication standpoint, many of the concepts suggested herein were utilized. For instance, the clinician assumed the responsibility of communicating with the other staff members. He approached them with a positive point of view rather than dwelling on what the student couldn't do in the class. He was, in all probability, empathetic or understanding of the problems the teacher was having and why she couldn't adapt to the student's individual needs. The clinician was reasonable in that he didn't indicate the problem was someone else's. The other staff members were reasonable in return. He was aggressive to the point that he stayed involved until something was done to improve the situation. However, most importantly he let the teacher and principal develop the solution to the problem and thus insured their cooperation and interest in its success.

## SUMMARY

The clinician working in a school setting conducts a program that is vastly different from the regular activities of the other personnel. The school staff probably does not understand the individualized methodology involved and may have a tendency to be only minimally supportive of the clinician and his program. In addition, many clinicians spend only a part of their day or week in a building, and as a result they are not looked upon as members of the staff. The results of this situation are often poor communications which tend to have a negative effect on the clinician and his program.

Communication and rapport become the responsibility of the clinician because of their importance to the effectiveness of his program. Therefore, when the clinician understands the concerns and goals of the other staff members and when he is willing to be the catalyst for the establishment of communication and the maintenance of rapport, he will find little difficulty in working with the educational staff in providing a meaningful program.

Good rapport and communications with the educational community are not difficult to establish and maintain. It does require effort. This effort is the responsibility of the clinician. It requires a knowledge of the motivations and concerns of other staff members. It requires a degree of reasonableness and perhaps some patience. It requires a bit of aggressiveness and cooperation from the other staff members. But most importantly, it requires a desire to be a part of the education of children.

## MATERIALS FOR DEVELOPMENT OF WRITING

*Imagine and Write:* My Weekly Reader, Education Center, Columbus, Ohio 43216, 1967.

*Imagine and Write* is a creative writing program for grades two through six. It develops vocabulary for writing, sensitivity to language, and awareness of literary forms. The program includes five, forty-eight page, paperback, consumable books, and teachers' guides. Emphasis is placed on creativity, not on the mechanics of writing.

*Paragraph Development:* Houghton Mifflin Co., 110 Tremont St., Boston, Mass. 02107, 1969.

Having a workbook-type format, this book provides exercises for improving paragraph writing. Lessons are included on identifying topic sentences, type of supporting sentences, methods of developing paragraphs, special purpose sentences and special purpose paragraphs.

*Sentence Improvement:* Houghton Mifflin Co., 110 Tremont St., Boston, Mass. 02107, 1971.

This book provides exercises which review basic sentence patterns and give practice in using phrases, clauses, parallel structures and modifiers. Following a workbook format, the book is intended for secondary school students.

*Stories You Can Finish:* American Education Publications, 55 High Street, Middletown, Conn. 06457, 1962.

This booklet, for use with junior high students, presents the beginnings of nine stories with just enough plot, character development, and setting to encourage students to complete their own versions. There are sections on editing stories at the end of each story which help students check specific elements of good story writing.

*Thinking and Writing: An Inductive Program in Composition:*
Prentice-Hall, Inc., Educational Book Division, Englewood Cliffs,
N. J. 07632, 1969.

This series of six student workbook-type texts and teachers'
editions was designed to teach children to write effectively in
grades one through six. *Thinking and Writing* presents sequen-
tially organized composition problems through which the children practice effective writing, develop thinking skills, and acquire concepts about the patterns and functions of language. A
bibliography is included which suggests supplementary reading
and sources of ideas for writing.

## MATERIALS FOR DEVELOPMENT OF VOCABULARY SKILLS

*In Other Words: A Beginning Thesaurus* and *In Other Words: A Junior Thesaurus:* Greet, W. Cabell, Jenkins, William A. and Schiller, A. Scott-Foresman and Company. Glenview, Illinois 60025.

Both of these exercise books are to be used in conjunction with their accompanying Scott-Foresman Thesaurus. The exercise booklets have three objectives. First, they offer substitutes for weary, worn-out, all purpose words by substituting about three thousand other words for about three hundred commonly used words. Second, they show children the shades of differences in meaning among synonyms; sample sentences are used for conveying precise meanings. Third, they are resource books for independent use by children. Various types of exercises including synonyms, antonyms, sentence fill-ins and completings, puzzles and others are included in the format.

*Know Your World:* A weekly newspaper, American Education Publications, Education Center, Columbus, Ohio.

A high interest, low reading newspaper geared to a second or third grade reading level.

*Looking at Words in Sentences:* White, Catherine E. and Taylor, Sanford E. (Eds.) EDL/McGraw-Hill Educational Developmental Laboratories, Inc. A Division of McGraw-Hill, Huntington, New York, 1970.

*Looking at Words* provides an instructional approach and materials in the vocabulary building area for word identification, word meanings in context, and structural analysis. Words taught in the *Looking at Words* program are taken from the EDL Core Vocabulary, a list based on a study of the frequency with which words appear in nine of the most popular based reading series. There are a series of workbooks each containing thirty lessons for levels four through six. The authors suggest the use of the tach-x and a filmstrip at each level.

*McGraw-Hill Vocabulary:* Sanford, Gene, McGraw-Hill, Inc. 1971, Huntington, New York.

*McGraw-Hill Vocabulary* is a series of booklets designed for secondary level students. It presents words which have use in the *real world*. It requires that the students learn only two words a day. After an explanation section, they are given two kinds of practice with the new words. In Exercise A, the student's ability to recognize meanings of words is tested. In Exercise B, the student's ability to recall the words and use them in a proper way is tested. The book also includes lessons to introduce the student to over forty Latin and Greek word parts upon which several hundred English words are based. Each booklet contains one hundred twenty lessons.

*Picto-cabulary Series:* Boning, Richard A., Barnell-Loft, Ltd., 958 Church Street, Baldwin, L. I., New York 11510.

This is a series of booklets to help enlarge vocabulary. The series features descriptive words. The words in each booklet are centered around a theme or topic. For example, one booklet, *Dense Forests and Majestic Mountains,* contains descriptive words about nature, such as *shimmering rivers, irregular coasts, balmy breezes.* Another booklet, for example, *Burly Athletes and Comely Girls,* contains descriptive words, such as, *a lean cowboy, a bedraggled lady,* and *a hefty weight lifter.* A test card is included for each booklet in the series.

*Word Bank:* The Mott Basic Language Skills Program, Chapman, Byrne E. and Schultz, Louis. Allied Education Council, Distribution Center, P. O. Box 78, Galien, Michigan 49113, 1969.

This is a workbook which contains three hundred photos of common objects with the association of a printed name written in both lower case print and in cursive writing. Each picture appears three times and is used each time in a different context. Each twenty-five word unit of vocabulary is used in narrative or story form to reinforce word recognition and spelling proficiency.

*Word Mastery:* Benner, Patricia Ann, New York, Houghton Mifflin Company, 53 West 43rd Street, New York, New York 10036.

Part of a series, *Troubleshooter,* it is designed to develop the student's knowledge of words at the secondary level. It is written for the student to proceed at his own speed. Each section includes a pretest, set A, review test A, and set B. If the student's score on Review Test A is below ninety percent, Review Test B is used. Each booklet has forty exercises for four complete lessons which are designed to teach homonyms, synonyms and antonyms.

*Wordly Wise:* Hodkinson, Kenneth and Ornato, Joseph C., Education Publishing Service, Inc., Cambridge, Mass., 1968.

This is a series of vocabulary booklets for secondary level students. Each booklet contains four exercises. The first exercise is a multiple-choice selection of closest meaning after study of multiple meanings from the glossary. The second and third exercises are correct usage in sentences, and the fourth exercise is a crossword puzzle. A teacher's key for each level accompanies the series.

*Words Are Important:* H. C. Hardwick Hammond Incorporated, Education Division, Maplewood, New Jersey 07040.

This is a series of vocabulary booklets for secondary level students for grades seven through college. The series is based on Thorndike and Lorge *Teachers' Word Book of 30,000 Words.* Each lesson consists of writing a paragraph using pre-selected words introduced in the lesson. Beginning with the third book, words which have been taught in previous books are reviewed. Each book contains eighteen lessons and review lessons.

*You and Your World:* A weekly newspaper, American Education Publications, Education Center, Columbus, Ohio.

A high interest, low reading newspaper geared to a fourth or fifth grade reading level.

## MATERIALS FOR DEVELOPMENT OF READING SKILLS

*Checkered Flag Series:* Field Educational Publications, Inc., 609 Mission Street, San Francisco, Calif. 94105, 1967.

This is a set of eight books ranging in reading level from 2.4 to 4.5, but of interest to students in the sixth through twelfth grades. All the books are about cars of various types and/or auto racing, therefore, making them interesting to most boys. Pre-recorded tapes, filmstrips and records are available for use with each book.

*Conquests in Reading:* Webster Division, McGraw-Hill Book Company, Manchester Road, Manchester, Mo. 63011, 1962.

This is a remedial workbook usable for students in the fourth through ninth grades. Phonetic analysis and structural analysis exercises are provided to improve reading and spelling skills. Vowel and consonant sounds are introduced through the book and the Dolch 220 basic sight words are incorporated. Short fables and stories with comprehension questions are provided which give the student practice using his newly acquired skills.

*Macmillan Reading Spectrum:* The Macmillan Co., 866 Third Avenue, New York, N. Y. 10022, 1964.

The Spectrum of Skills set includes booklets entitled, *Word Analysis, Vocabulary Development* and *Reading Comprehension* at each of six levels. The booklets are intended for use beginning in the intermediate grades. There is an accompanying Spectrum of Books which may also be used.

*New Reading Skill Builders:* Reader's Digest Services, Inc., Educational Division, Pleasantville, N. Y. 10570, 1969.

The primary kit includes books for students reading at the first through fourth grade reading levels; intermediate, from second through sixth; and advanced from fourth through tenth. Stories and exercises are presented in each book.

*Sullivan Programmed Readers:* Webster Division, McGraw-Hill Book Co., Manchester Road, Manchester, Mo. 63011, 1966.

This is a basal reading program for use in the primary grades which can also be used in a corrective program for the middle and upper grades. The paper-bound books incorporate an individualized, programmed approach for the teaching of reading. The content is highly motivating for students of elementary school age.

*Read-Study-Think:* My Weekly Reader, Education Center, Columbus, Ohio 43216, 1970.

Short illustrated articles are followed by reading comprehension, vocabulary, thinking and organizational exercises. Five booklets are available for use with children in grades two through six.

*Reading for Concepts:* Webster Division, McGraw-Hill Book Co., Manchester Road, Manchester, Mo. 63011, 1970.

This is an eight-volume reading comprehension series usable with students in the third to twelfth grades. Reading levels range from 1.6 to 6.8, which makes the series fall in the high interest, low reading level group and appropriate for remedial readers. Exercises are provided to improve comprehension and to build skill in drawing conclusions and making inferences.

*Reading for Meaning:* J. B. Lippincott Co., East Philadelphia Square, Philadelphia, Pa. 19105, 1962.

*Reading for Meaning* consists of a series of workbooks ranging in difficulty from fourth grade to twelfth grade level. Stories have been rated by students in the appropriate grades, and the stories included in the series were found to be most interesting. Each short story, of approximately half a page in length, is followed by exercises on word meanings, title selection, main idea, recalling facts, outlining and making inferences.

*Specific Skills Series:* Barnell-Loft, Ltd., 958 Church Street, Baldwin, L. I., N. Y. 11510, 1970.

Booklets include exercises in seven skill areas, *Getting the Main Idea, Using the Context, Working with Sounds, Following Directions, Locating the Answer, Getting the Facts* and *Drawing Conclusions.* Booklets are provided for each of the six elementary grades in each skill area. Lessons are short and interest sustaining but mature in format. A value of the series is that several exercises at increasing levels of difficulty are provided so a student may be given frequent but varied practice on the particular skill areas with which he needs help.

*Study Exercises for Developing Reading Skills:* Laidlaw Brothers, Thatcher and Madison, River Forest, Ill. 60305, 1965.

The authors suggest that the four books in this series be used for remedial work, books A and B for the elementary grades and books C and D for junior high. Exercises are included for improving comprehension and vocabulary, learning to use the dictionary, interpreting prose and poetry, and reading for utilitarian purposes.

# NAME INDEX

Anderson, V. A., 70

Baer, C. J., 58
Balow, B., 115
Barley, M., 159
Barnhart, C. L., 114
Blackwood, R. O., 88
Bond, G. L., 115
Bruner, F. G., 52
Butts, D. S., 157

Carhart, R., 56, 70
Cattell, N. R., 104
Chomsky, C., 106, 132
Chreist, F. M., 157
Costello, M. R., 62
Cozad, R. L., 10, 20, 26, 27

Darley, F. L., 10, 12, 16, 17, 100, 108
Davis, H., 52, 53, 54, 70
Day, H. E., 56
Doerfler, L. G., 15
Doster, M. E., 10, 15
Downs, M. P., 10, 15

Eagles, E. L., 15, 23
Eisenson, J., 52, 58
Eisenstadt, A. A., 90
Elser, R. P., 58

Fisher, B., 58
Frackenpohl, H., 144
Fusfeld, I. S., 56

Gaeth, J. H., 61, 62, 63, 65
Gates, A. I., 115
Gates, R., 63, 65
Gendel, E., 10, 26, 27
Goetzinger, C. P., 58, 61

Harrison, C., 58
Hoyt, C., 115
Hudgins, C. V., 62, 65

Jeffers, J., 159
Johnson, W., 99, 100, 108

Kelly, J. C., 62

Lane, K., 146
Lev, J., 57, 60
Levine, H. S., 15, 23
Lowell, E., 155

MacGinite, W. H., 115
MacMillan, D. P., 52
McConnell, F., 58, 59
McNeill, D., 56
Manger, R. F., 89, 112, 124
Melnick, W., 15, 23
Mott, A. J., 52
Myklebust, H. R., 112

Newby, H., 70

Paterson, D. G., 52
Pintner, R., 52, 56, 57, 58, 60
Pipe, P., 122
Prall, J., 62
Presler, M. J., 14
Purcell, G., 62

Reamer, J. C., 56

Sanders, D. A., 62, 65
Schloesser, P., 10, 26, 27
Silverman, S. R., 52, 54, 70
Sivian, L. J., 53, 54
Smith, J. L., 52
Spriesterbach, D. C., 100, 108
Stanton, M., 52, 58
Stewart, J. L., 14
Stoner, M., 155
Streng, A. H., 104, 132
Stuckless, E. R., 63

Taylor, H., 52

209

# SUBJECT INDEX

## A

Abilities, functional, 6
Achievement tests
  monitoring growth, 118
  standardized, 94
  usefulness of vocabulary subsections, 118-119
Acoustic room, 20
Adenoids, hypertrophied, 39
Advancements, medical and surgical, problems created by, 50
Affixes, noun-plural, misusage, 96
Allergic problem, 39
American National Standards Institute (ANSI), 13, 18, 20, 54
American Standard Association (ASA), 17, 18, 53
Amplification, 93, 98
  classroom, 169
  classroom, Fig., 168
  difficulty tolerating, 74
  introduction to, 180-181
  speech production, 82
Antibiotics, 50
Antihistaminic drugs, 39
Articulation, 95
Articulation problems, 98
Audiological information, predicting speech errors, 73-84
Audiologist, hearing aid evaluation, 177, 180
Audiometer
  earphones, 54
  model 2A, 54
  screening, 13-15
Audiometer norm, relationship ASA to ISO, 18, 54
Auditory discrimination ability, 162, 176

Auditory sensitivity, 162
Auditory training, 152-157
  defined, 152
  factors in providing, 152-153
  methods and materials, 154-156
  nursery rhymes, 156
  popular music, 156
  role of amplification in, 153-154
Auditory patterning, 133
Auricle, role in hearing, 32

## B

Bacteria, 43
Behavioral objectives, 89, 121
  defined, 124
  examples of, 124-125
  steps in writing, 124

## C

Cerumen
  hearing loss, 32-33
  purpose of, 32, 34
Chicken pox, 49
Child, normal, habilitation of, 3-4
Cholesteatoma, 31, 41
Class rosters, 24
Classroom seating, 154
Classroom teacher, 153, 191
Cleft palate, 38
Clergy, 4
Clinician
  habilitation team, 5
  self-concept, 191
  total educational program, 189
Communication
  aggressiveness, 196-197
  basis of poor, 190-192
  cooperation, 197

211

educational level, 150-151
emphasis in therapy, 88
factors affecting language, 95
family support, 151-152
language acquisition, 93
language problems, 93-95
learning, 61-65
social and emotional adjustment, 150
speech errors, 94
steps in habilitating, 31
vocabulary concepts, 94
written language, 94
Hearing impairment
nonreversible, 28
variables related to, 54-57
Hearing loss
age of onset, 56-57, 149
alleviation of, 6
classification of, 32
conductive, 162
common causes in students, 35
definition of, 32
effect on speech development, 76-79
importance of medical exam, 78
influence on vocal quality and intensity, 77-78
maximum loss, 57
moderate bilateral, Fig., 77
use of amplification with, 78-79
etiology, importance in learning, 149
incidence from screening by grade level, 10
measurable psychological problems, 54
sensorineural, 162
acquired, 47-50
bilateral, high frequency, Fig., 78
bilateral, moderate-to-severe, Fig., 81
classification of, 47
etiology, 47
hereditary, 47
(high frequency), effect on speech production, 79-80
identifying causes of, 47
(mild-to-moderate), effect on speech production, 80-84

(mild-to-severe), high frequency, Fig., 80
(more severe from low-to-high frequency), Fig., 83
peri-natal causes, 47-49
post-natal causes, 49-50
sharply dropping, Fig., 75
site of lesion, 47
severity, effect on speech and language development, 149-150
symptom, 6
type of, 57
unilateral, effect on learning, 35
unilateral, effect on speech development, 76
Hearing screening
inclusiveness and frequency of, 9-10
medical referral form, 27
new students, 10-11
referral and follow up, 26-27
rescreening, last year's failures, 10
selected portion or entire class, 9
test environment, 19-21
test site, 19-20
tests, 11-13
Hearing screening program
class roster, Fig., 24
comprehensiveness of, 9-11
coordination of, 26
informing parents, physicians and school staff, 21-22
moving students to and from test area, 22-23
organization of, 21-26
planning screening, 22-23
recording results, 23-24
records of, 28
rescreening, 23
teachers informational letter, Fig., 25
test setting, 23
Hearing screening test
criteria for failure, 18-19
criteria, philosophy in selection of, 15
failure by normal hearing, 19
frequency criteria, 15-17
intensity criteria, 17-18
rescreening criteria, 18